CALAVERAS HEAD START
& STATE PRESCHOOL
Post Office Box 1225
Valley Springs, California 95252

# Hollyhocks and

## Honeybees

### Garden Projects for Young Children

**Sara Starbuck, Marla Olthof, and Karen Midden**

Redleaf Press
St. Paul, Minnesota
www.redleafpress.org

Illustrations by Karen Midden

Published by:  Redleaf Press
a division of Resources for Child Caring
450 N. Syndicate, Suite 5
St. Paul, MN 55104

Library of Congress Cataloging-in-Publication Data

Starbuck, Sara, 1955–
    Hollyhocks and honeybees : garden projects for young children / by
Sara Starbuck, Marla Olthof, and Karen Midden.
    p. cm.
    Includes bibliographical references and index.
    ISBN 1-929610-20-3
    1. School gardens. 2. Children's gardens. 3. Gardening—Experiments.
4. Gardening—Study and teaching—Activity programs. I. Olthof, Marla,
1970– II. Midden, Karen, 1952– III. Title.
SB55 .S78 2002
372.3'5—dc21
                                                        2002002689


Printed in Canada

*To my parents, who gave me roots and wings;*
*McCartney, who gives me hope;*
*And Charles, the mirror to my soul.*

SARA

*To Jesus Christ, my Lord. Thank you for the*
*opportunity to serve you by working with your*
*precious children.*

*To my parents. You are my first teachers. From*
*you I have learned to serve God, value family,*
*and put my whole heart into my work.*

*To Todd, my husband. Thank you for always*
*supporting my goals and dreams. I love you!*

*And to my little peapod, Haleigh. Your life has*
*given mine a new perspective. You are my*
*favorite project!*

MARLA

*To all the young children who find adventure*
*and joy exploring a garden and to their teachers*
*and parents who join in.*

*Also, to my daughters, Lonzie and Nyssa; my*
*husband, Chris; and my parents, Bob and Theda*
*Stoelzle, who share their explorations with me and*
*have taught me so much.*

KAREN

# Contents

# Acknowledgments

Our adventures in gardening would never have taken place, nor would we have written this book, without the assistance of many people. Our gratitude to these friends and colleagues is immense. Listed here are only a few of those involved:

Jessica Chambers, whose dedication above and beyond her master's thesis requirements brought our garden to life. We also thank Jessica for the use of her photographs, some of which we share in this book.

Bruce Francis and the grounds maintenance department of the Southern Illinois University physical plant, who donated time, labor, and materials, without which we could not have developed our extensive garden. They continue to support us in maintaining our garden area.

Many Child Development Laboratories (CDL) parents and staff, as well as early childhood, landscape, and horticulture students, have contributed time, energy, and materials to our garden projects over the years. Their contributions are monumental.

Lori Huffman of the University Museum arranged for the loan and installation of the sculpture that graces our sensory garden.

Many local businesses contributed to our garden. Special thanks go to Steve and Bonnie Bailey, former owners of Family Tree Nursery, for supporting us in our fieldwork. Thanks to Sunflower Landscaping, which donated many of the plants that live in our garden.

A number of our early childhood students have assisted us in explorations of the garden with children. Their participation and education have enriched the process and this book. Special thanks to Liz Collins for her photographs and to those students who are pictured in this book.

Bernie Weithorn and Leigh Bodokis also shot beautiful photographs for this book.

Kelly Ricketts, Karen Olthof, Marla Mallette, and Susan Pearlman were helpful in proofreading the manuscript and providing feedback. Special thanks goes to Sara's husband, Charles Rudolph, who has probably read this book more times than we have. He is a master at relocating commas and scouting out the perfect word for tired authors.

Barbara Eichholz, our mentor and a former CDL teacher, provided baby-sitting services for young Haleigh, as did Carrie Dekker and Marla's mom, June DeWerff. Their patience is much appreciated!

Beth Wallace, our editor, has been supportive and encouraging every step of the way.

The CDL kids, many of whom appear in the photographs of this book, have guided us in our education about gardening with children. They taught us all we know. We love them deeply and carry them in our hearts.

# Introduction

This book is the work of three women—one a parent, one a teacher, and one the director—at the Child Development Laboratories (CDL) at Southern Illinois University Carbondale (SIUC). Southern Illinois University Carbondale is located in extreme southern Illinois, 350 miles south of Chicago. The Child Development Laboratories are part of the Department of Curriculum and Instruction within the College of Education and Human Services at SIUC. CDL provides half-day and full-day care to children six weeks to six years of age. It also serves as a teacher-training facility for students enrolled in Early Childhood Education and provides opportunities for research for faculty members and students. Gardening has been part of the curriculum at CDL since the early nineties. The garden highlighted in this book was built in 1997. Through this book, we hope to share with you not only the joy but also the intellectual depth that gardening has brought to the curriculum at CDL.

Sara Starbuck has been the director of CDL since 1992. Before that, she was the preschool master teacher there for seven years. Marla Olthof was the preschool master teacher at CDL from 1993 to 1998, during the years that the garden was developed there. Karen Midden is a landscape architect and an associate professor in Plant and Soil Science at SIUC. Her two daughters, Lonzie and Nyssa, attended CDL from infancy until they started kindergarten.

In 1996 Karen approached Sara about starting a garden at CDL. Karen had come across a grant application and thought we might be able to get funding to help us start the garden. Karen also introduced Sara and Marla to Jessica Chambers, a master's student in Plant and Soil Science. Jessica researched children's gardens and came up with a wonderful design that would actually incorporate a number of children's gardens into our playground. We sent off the grant application and waited.

We waited a long time and, in fact, never did hear a word. However, Jessica was invested in building the garden as the focus for her master's thesis and the rest of us were determined to get the garden off the ground. We decided to build as much as we could afford of the gardens Jessica had designed.

Our goal was to develop a garden that provided diversity: areas for vegetables and flowers, areas for quiet play, and opportunities for exploration. We wanted to invite insects, frogs, butterflies, and bunnies into our garden. We also wanted to share the beauty of our garden with all the people who passed by our playground. However, our space had definite limitations. The CDL facility and playground is located on the north side of a four-story building. Between the shade from the building and the large trees on the playground, we have few areas that receive sufficient sun for a garden. We determined that the best space was on the east side of the playground along the fence. Although this space left us with a long, narrow garden, most of it would get enough sun for flowers and vegetables.

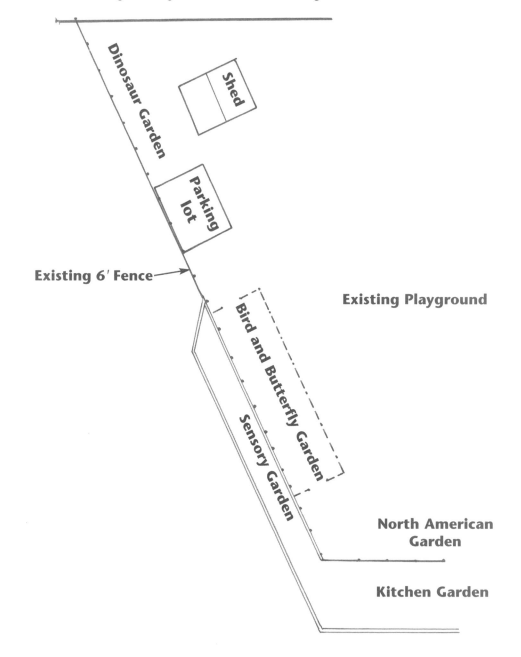

We decided to place part of the garden inside the fence, where children would have constant access; we would place the other part outside the fence, where the children would need to be accompanied by a teacher. To develop our space to the best advantage, we chose to break up the length of the area by incorporating several themes, developing smaller gardens within the large garden area. We ended up with a dinosaur garden, a bird and butterfly garden, a North American garden, a kitchen garden, and five separate sensory gardens—one each for taste, smell, touch, hearing, and seeing. Suggestions for each of these gardens are included in chapter 3.

Since we're at a university with union laborers, we didn't have the flexibility that many schools have in building the garden. A family workday was out of the question. Fortunately, however, we were able to gain cooperation from Bruce Francis in the SIUC Grounds Department and his staff. They offered to donate their time and some materials to get us going. Since we were not allowed to do any carpentry work, we bought the biggest pieces of wood we could find (10 inches by 10 inches by 10 feet) for the boundaries of the raised bed. The grounds crew put these in place, donated topsoil and compost, tilled the ground, and got us ready to go.

We began searching for donations. We wrote to seed companies, enclosing a list of seeds we needed, and we visited local businesses to ask for contributions. We made a list of plants we wanted, ranging from the inexpensive to more costly shrubs, and posted it in our lobby along with a request that parents donate one of the items listed. We approached other parents for specific tasks. One of our fathers, who taught art, made models of a dinosaur footprint and created molds for stepping-stones. Karen took these molds to one of her classes and, over a period of time, her students made enough footprints to fill the dinosaur garden. Another father, who also taught art, had previously provided us with dinosaur sculptures made of rebar. These were originally covered with chicken wire and papier-mâché. Now they had been stripped back to the original rebar and would be used as trellises in the dinosaur garden.

We ordered some seeds that we didn't think would be donated, and a couple of companies sent boxes of the seeds we had requested. Jessica started these at the greenhouse. Her husband, Jason, built a trellis house for the North American garden. A CDL mother scouted around the university until she found some bricks that weren't being used and secured permission for us to use them in our bird and butterfly garden. Other parents donated bird feeders, birdhouses, and gardening books, sometimes in honor of a child's birthday. One mother agreed to paint the signs that would be posted to identify each of the gardens. Karen's class donated their time to help us install heavy materials and plant the garden.

The preschoolers, who had raised money from crushing and selling soft-drink cans, voted to buy a butterfly house for the garden. And a parent who was the curator for the University Museum arranged for the donation and installation of a sculpture in the sensory garden. In the end, we received so much cooperation that very little of our original plan had to be scuttled.

We've taken the garden through a few summers now, and it continues to bring joy into our lives and those of our children. We have learned much and continue to learn as we involve our children in gardening. Sometimes children who have moved on to elementary school return to visit, and they often fondly recall their time spent in our garden. This book was written to share with others just a bit of what we have gleaned from our experiences.

# 1

# Why Garden?

Children are drawn to nature. They long to be outdoors. There, they caress the fuzzy lamb's ears growing in the garden, blow delicate dandelion puffs and watch them shatter and the seeds drift away on the wind, giggle as caterpillars crawl tickling up their arms.

Gardening offers everything a teacher could want when developing curriculum to draw children into their world. As in other fertile curriculum topics, gardening provides opportunities for children to develop socially and emotionally, individually and as a community. The work involved in gardening supports children's physical development, nourishes all their senses, and helps them learn to slow down and observe carefully. In addition, the knowledgeable teacher can use gardening as a basis for a full intellectual curriculum, incorporating language and literacy, science and math concepts, social sciences, and the arts. Finally, gardening offers a unique opportunity for teachers to foster dispositions, or "habits of mind," such as curiosity, cooperativeness, respect for living things, persistence, and caring, that will serve children well throughout their lives (Katz 1993, 6).

## Physical, Social, and Emotional Development

Young children are sensory learners, and gardening calls to all their senses. The visual impact of flowers, vegetables, and living creatures pulls them into the garden, where they immediately reach out to touch the growing plants. They notice the

fragrance of flowers and herbs, hear the grasses rustle in the wind and the hum of the bumblebee as she settles on a coneflower. They pick mint, perhaps tasting the herb for the first time in its natural state. Later, they harvest vegetables and herbs to use in cooking activities, and maybe try a food for the first time because they grew it themselves.

Gardening is movement and children need to move. They can't help it. Ask a group of three-year-olds to sit still, then observe how much harder this is for them than running and climbing. We've always known that movement helps bodies grow, and now researchers have confirmed that it is also necessary for brain development.

The garden gives children a place to practice both fine and gross motor skills with purpose. Children dig holes to plant seeds or seedlings. They pick up tiny seeds and place them in a hole or broadcast them carefully over a wide space. They collect mulch in wheelbarrows and spread it on the garden, then hold the hose as they sprinkle water over the growing plants. Weeding requires careful selection and removal of unwanted plants. Picking flowers takes skill and practice: pull too hard and the roots come up, cut too high up and there

is no stem to put in the vase. Some flowers can be broken off; some need to be cut with scissors. When the children harvest vegetables, they must use just the right amount of pressure in removing the desired part of the plant to avoid damaging the remaining part.

Social growth occurs when children work in groups in the garden. They learn to listen to each other and share what they know. Because their experiences differ, they learn from each other. They develop social skills as they encounter situations that involve taking turns, compromising, and sharing. Patience and the ability to tolerate delays evolve as children learn that their turn does come when they work cooperatively with others.

Children and adults all have to work cooperatively in the garden. This is a group project, and negotiation is sometimes necessary when determining what to grow, who will do what task, how to carry out a needed job, or

what to do with the harvest. Everyone has to work together to solve problems when they occur, building a sense of teamwork.

Children develop confidence as they work in the garden. They conquer fears as they encounter new creatures in their explorations, examine them, hold them in their hands, and return them to their homes. Even children who don't like to get dirty are drawn to a session of planting flowers. They dig with trowels and, though they may don gloves or grab the stem of the plant to avoid touching the soil, they participate. The garden is responsive to children with disabilities or to those who are just learning the common language of their school. Many plants take very little skill to grow, and a good teacher can include everyone.

Gardens are beautiful. Many teachers in recent years have begun to recognize that institutional-style buildings and classrooms lack the aesthetic qualities that are necessary to foster a deep appreciation of life in children. Adding a garden softens the outdoor classroom area and adds a focal point that changes the quality of the playground experience. By bringing flowers or foliage cuttings from the garden inside, children and teachers can do the same for the indoor classroom.

Anyone who enjoys gardening knows the sense of calm that comes from handling soil, tucking seedlings tenderly away, watching the plants and animals that inhabit the garden.

The garden demands that people wait. Plants grow at their own pace. The garden gives children opportunities to slow down and take time to explore in detail. Children who observe closely will notice small changes from day to day, large changes from week to week. They learn the need for patience and careful observation. They learn to nurture.

With gardening, teachers can create private spaces for children. Much has been written about the need for children who are in group programs for much of the day to have some privacy. In fact, while teachers occasionally take breaks, children are usually not allowed to leave the classroom. They are often expected to remain with a large group of other people for nine hours a day, or even longer. As adults, we know the importance of building in time to be alone, to think, to observe from a distance. Garden spaces can give children this opportunity. Teachers can build a special structure (such as a trellis house) with this end in mind, or plant so that small, protective spaces are left. Whether the space is under a low-hanging tree, behind a bush, between rows of plantings, or within a carefully constructed sunflower house, children will appreciate the joining of solitude with the comfort of natural elements.

## Integrated Learning

A garden makes an excellent project for a classroom. A careful teacher can incorporate all areas of academic learning into the garden project, keeping the children's interest and enthusiasm alive over the period of time it takes the garden to complete its cycle.

Science is the most obvious area of learning associated with gardening, and the garden is rich in science learning. It would be impossible to list all the science concepts that can be included in a garden project. Of course, children will observe plant growth and life cycles. When gardening, they also learn about the entire garden ecosystem. Once they have planted, the children and teachers must contend with weeds, insufficient rainfall, and pests. They also observe other animals that are attracted to the garden, such as large bumblebees, butterflies, and birds. They learn about creatures such as worms, which are useful in a garden. Other creatures have little impact on the growth of the plants, but are interesting to study. For example, some children will spend hours examining pill bugs they've dug up from under a rock or log.

Although gardening is a method of controlling the environment, it does present elements of the natural environment to children. Children gain an appreciation for the environment when they are exposed to nature. This awareness at an early age is necessary if children are to grow into adults who care about the environment, who see how we are connected to the earth in the most primal ways. Ask any adult who cares intensely about acting responsibly toward the environment and she will be able to tell stories of how she bonded with nature at a young age. When we garden with children, we allow them to become responsible for a small part of their world and give them the opportunity to connect with the earth and its creatures. Through gardening, children begin to make the connection between what is sold in the supermarkets and the earth from which it comes. They begin to see their place in the ecological web that is our world.

The most obvious learning from a garden may be in the area of science, but the garden also offers tremendous opportunities for language development. Even adults will learn new vocabulary words as they explore gardening with children. Children love repeating complicated Latin names, as well as identifying such colorfully named plants as "dragon's blood sedum," "New Guinea impatiens," "mammoth Russian sunflower," and "birdhouse gourd." They will

also need to communicate as they plan and complete tasks, make observations, and record their findings. Literacy skills develop as children read books, do research, label plants, follow recipes, and make representations of what they see.

Children use math skills often when they work in the garden. They count seeds as they plant, using one-to-one correspondence, if they are placing seeds in individual containers. They observe growth and may measure certain plants—for instance, comparing the size of the giant sunflower to other objects in their environment or even to themselves. They classify as they observe and record data, often graphing their findings and drawing conclusions. When the time comes to prepare food from the garden, children count and classify, compare size, and measure as they follow recipes.

The garden readily lends itself to exploration through the arts. Children construct images from the garden through drawing, painting, and modeling. The teacher can introduce songs and finger plays about gardening. Children respond readily to creative movement and dramatic experiences that revolve around the garden. For example, they grow like trees, fly like birds, sway in the wind like tall flowers.

With the study of gardening, children also begin learning what primary teachers call "social studies." They look beyond their own garden to other gardens in the community. They may visit related businesses, such as greenhouses, nurseries, florists, and produce markets. They begin to understand the economic web of a community, and they make connections with community members.

Perhaps the most important contribution of gardening to the curriculum is that it offers an opportunity to encourage dispositions in children that create sensitive, caring, lifelong learners (Katz 1993). In the garden, curiosity, initiative, and responsibility are rewarded. Because children are eager to explore, they are rewarded with discoveries. Because they choose to work, the work is enjoyable and they continue to choose it. Because their continued efforts pay off, they learn the value of accountability. Children become resourceful as they explore ways to accomplish tasks or solve problems. They learn that persistence pays off, as they try new solutions and eventually experience success. As they learn more about the creatures in the garden, they develop sensitivity and respect for others.

## Using the Project Approach with Gardening

At the Child Development Laboratories, we use the "project approach" in designing our curriculum. This teaching style, like that of the Reggio Emilia schools in Italy, enables teachers to immerse children in a topic of interest over an extended period of time while integrating various disciplines, such as science, language arts, social studies, math, and the fine arts. During a project, children actively engage in learning and in sharing their new knowledge with others. This approach creates a community of learners in which every member's contribution is valued. Those contributions may come in the form of questions, observations, background experience, or representation of thoughts and ideas. Lilian Katz (1994, 1) defines the project approach:

> A project is an in-depth investigation of a topic worth learning more about. The investigation is usually undertaken by a small group of children within a class, sometimes by a whole class, and occasionally by an individual child. The key feature of a project is that it is a research effort deliberately focused on finding answers to questions about a topic posed either by the children, the teacher, or the teacher working with the children. The goal of a project is to learn more about the topic rather than to seek right answers to questions posed by the teacher.

A project differs from a theme or a unit in that it is child-driven. The teacher begins with what the children already know, focuses on the interests of the children through conversation and observation, and helps children identify and find answers to their questions through their own investigations.

Gardens lend themselves well to the project format because of their complexity and the variety of different ways in which children can become involved. Through gardening, children have the opportunity to discover the immediate and useful connections between science, math, literacy, and social studies. The learning gained through this type of project will be continuously meaningful and relevant in their everyday lives. In addition, with the variety of tasks involved in creating and maintaining a garden, there is something to capture the interest of every child in the group.

If you are interested in using the project approach in your classroom we recommend two books. *The Project Approach: Making Curriculum Come Alive* (Chard 1998) gives a quick overview of the project approach. *Young Investigators: The Project Approach in the Early Years* (Helm and Katz 2001) is more detailed and includes a journal that you can use as you work your way through the process.

## The Role of the Teacher

Teachers initially may be hesitant to take on a classroom garden, particularly if they haven't had any personal experience with gardening. They may question whether they know enough about growing plants to teach children. In this section, we will discuss what the teacher needs to know before beginning a garden project (or more accurately, what dispositions a teacher needs to have). We will also explain the importance of planning for experiences that retain intellectual integrity, focusing on concepts, creating a concept web and using it to document work in the classroom, integrating all aspects of the curriculum into the garden project, and asking questions that help children think and learn.

## What the Teacher Needs to Know

The best thing about gardening with children is that anyone can do it. Even if you've never planted a seed, you have what it takes as long as you have a positive attitude and the will to

learn. When we started our garden, only Karen had a real horticultural background. Sara's gardening experience was limited to small projects with preschool children and growing roses at home. And, although Marla had grown up on a farm and worked in gardens with her parents and grandparents as a child, at the time our project began she didn't garden at all. Fortunately, teachers of young children don't need to have a lot of knowledge at the beginning. What you need is authentic interest that drives your explorations as you learn with the children. You should be able to admit when you don't know something, as you guide children in search of answers. With such modeling, children will be able to ask questions freely.

We can make two promises. First, no matter what your level of expertise, you will learn something new from experiencing gardening with children. Second, you will learn much more from your failures than you will from your successes, as long as you're willing to try again when things don't work out as you had hoped.

As a teacher, you must be a role model of interest and curiosity. Your enthusiasm is essential if you want the children to be enthusiastic. And you must express a sense of wonder if the children are to be free to express the same. This shouldn't be hard. Even avid gardeners still feel that sense of awe when a shrub first begins to bud after winter dormancy or when a ½-inch seed produces a 10-foot sunflower.

Joseph Cornell, in *Sharing Nature with Children* (1979, 11), suggests "Teach less, and share more." This is the best possible advice for a teacher of young children. You can do this by telling stories about your experiences with nature. Talk about your *feelings*, rather than what you know. Express the amazement you feel. Take cues from the children. Find the delight that exists within you and share it. Express your disappointment when things don't turn out well. Follow that up with the determination to try again. Provide abundant resource materials and use them constantly. When you find a new insect, get out an insect reference book and look it up. You'll find children will spend long stretches of time exploring well-designed reference books. For instance, after looking up cicadas and Japanese beetles with a teacher, two of our children spent another thirty minutes looking through the book *Bugs* (Lowenstein and Lechner 1999).

You are the key to a successful project. You need not know all the answers, but must be curious, interested, and willing to help search for answers. The garden should not be seen as a list of plant names to be memorized or characteristics to be studied. Avoid trying to fill the children with information and following up with questions to test their knowledge. It's less important for children to learn facts about the garden than it is for them to develop concepts. The children will learn naturally when they are intensely involved. They will become intensely involved when you are able to model enthusiasm and respond to their cues.

Be willing to let children explore incorrect answers. Part of the scientific experience is testing hypotheses and dismissing them. Don't be in a hurry to dismiss the child's conclusion. Hands-on experience with gardening is crucial to the young child's understanding of scientific concepts, and the best approach is to view it as research. Some plants will not grow well, while others will flourish. Some will become bug infested or be devoured by rabbits and squirrels. This is all part of the process of investigation. Our role as teachers is to guide children so that these seemingly unsuccessful experiments become meaningful learning opportunities.

Dying or half-eaten plants often leave children with many questions, "What happened to the lettuce?" or, "How can we get rid of these slugs?" As adults, we often have answers handy, offering them quickly to children. However, we provide a better learning experience for children if we let them lead by asking them to create some sort of hypothesis: "You know, that is a very good question. What do you think happened to our lettuce? Have you seen any visitors in this part of the garden lately? What do you think might have happened?"

Allowing children to make predictions adds to their learning. Once children have given it some thought, you can discuss ways to verify their predictions: "Would you like to set aside some time tomorrow to sit quietly and observe the vegetable garden to see if you are right?" or, "Maybe you could interview the other teachers and children to see if they have seen any critters in this part of the garden." Once the children have more experience conducting these types of projects, you can simply ask, "How do you think we could find out more about what has been going on with the lettuce?" The child's response will provide information about his developmental level and problem-solving abilities.

Be willing to take things slowly. Observe the children. Cherish the time it takes to get down to the children's level, nose-to-nose with a dandelion, if necessary. Stop to see what has caught the children's attention. Focus their attention on new sights and sounds. Your role is a crucial one because children are very sensitive to what is important to adults. If the natural world is important to you, it will become important to the children. Keep in mind that a sense of joy should permeate the gardening experience. If gardening becomes a set of chores, the children will back off and your project will fail. If your garden is very large, the children will not be able to do all the work. We realized early on that parents and staff would need to find time for weeding because our garden is so large. The children do enjoy weeding and they do weed, but they are never forced to do so. It is treated as an enjoyable activity. Don't worry if not everyone participates in the work or shows a great deal of interest in gardening. The children will benefit from simply being near the garden, watching tiny seedlings develop into beautiful plants, playing under dancing flowers while butterflies float on the breeze and bumblebees zip past their ears.

This book tells you everything you need to get started. While we won't give you all the answers, we will share basic information with you and give you ideas for activities to try. You will discover much on your own as you and the children take a journey into the world of gardening.

## Assuring Intellectual Integrity

If we are to do our best for children, we must plan for their intellectual development. It is easy for us to fall back on curriculum that is "cute" or "fun," without regard to what the children are actually learning. Katz and Chard (1993, 4) stress the need to focus on intellectual goals when planning curriculum. They believe that "children's minds should be engaged in ways that deepen their understanding of their own experiences and environment," and add that "the younger the children, the more important it is that most of the activities provided for them engage their intellects."

It is easy, in designing experiences for the young learner, to dilute the message or even to provide information that is inaccurate or confusing to the child. In *Reaching Potentials: Appropriate Curriculum and Assessment for Young Children* (1992, 39), Sue Bredekamp relates a story about an experience from early in her teaching career. She had planned what she thought was a "cute" activity: cutting the tops off potatoes, replacing them with cotton balls, and planting grass seed on top to simulate hair. Although she enthusiastically checked on the progress of the "potato-

head faces" each morning, she noticed that the children were not interested in the project. After reevaluating the activity, she concluded, "Grass doesn't grow on cotton balls, grass doesn't grow on potatoes, and potatoes don't grow hair! It seems fortunate that the children did *not* engage with this project because if they had, it is hard to imagine what learning would have resulted and what relationship that learning would have had to reality." (Bredekamp and Rosegrant 1992, 39)

Any veteran teacher can tell such stories. This is why it is so important that whenever words such as "cute" come to mind, we ask ourselves what the child will actually learn from the activity. If we cannot find value in the activity beyond this adjective, if we cannot determine what concepts the child will be learning from the activity, or if the learning is not true to the academic discipline the activity springs from, then it is likely that the activity does not have intellectual integrity.

In addition to learning, we also want children to enjoy their work in the classroom. But in the same way we want to avoid "cute" as a criterion for curriculum, we also want to avoid planning activities just because they are fun for the children. For example, picking all the flowers from the garden and throwing them in the air might be fun for the children, but would likely fail to teach them anything meaningful. Katz and Chard (1993, 5) state, "While enjoyment is a desirable goal for entertainment, it is not an appropriate aim of education. A major aim of education is to improve the learners' understanding of the world around them and to strengthen their dispositions to go on learning. When educational practices succeed in doing so, learners find their experiences enjoyable. But enjoyment is a side effect or by-product of being engaged in worthwhile activity, effort, and learning."

Through a garden project, children are guided in scientific discoveries, not encouraged to believe in magical thinking. For instance, it would be easy to let children believe that the beanstalk grew because the beans were magic, but it would not be true to the discipline of science.

In addition, we must consider the developmental level of the involved children, the relationship of the curriculum to the world that they know, and their ability to participate actively in their learning. To be appropriate for young children, curriculum must be presented in a manner that respects their intelligence while adapting to their ability levels and their knowledge about and relationship to the world around them.

To evaluate an activity for intellectual integrity and appropriateness, ask yourself the following questions:

- What is the concept behind this activity? (If you have difficulty naming a concept, the activity is possibly frivolous and not worthy of the children's time and attention.)
- Is the activity of interest to the child?
- Is the information that will be presented worth knowing?
- Is the information that this activity presents accurate and credible?
- Can the information be presented to these children in a manner that is meaningful to them?
- If the content is related to a discipline, such as math or science, is it true to the knowledge base of the discipline?
- If the content involves literature, poetry, art, or music, is the work of recognized quality?
- Can the children relate this activity to what is real in their lives and the world they know?
- Will children be involved actively in the learning process?

## Focusing on Concepts

It is a teacher's job to determine what to teach. While it is easy to focus on facts, and parents often respond positively when children are able to recite a series of facts, the simple memorization and regurgitation of information does not attest to real learning. Indeed, many preschoolers can recite the alphabet or numbers from one to twenty without having any understanding of what they represent. Facts change and become outdated with time. Think about information you memorized as a child that no longer holds true. Science marches on, disproving what was once considered certainty. In addition, some facts are simply not worth knowing. Most adults can conjure up some memorized material from early in their primary schooling that has been of little use since. The value of filling up children's heads with

information and asking them to repeat it back is questionable, at best. At a minimum, facts must connect to the child's world in a meaningful way to be useful.

On the other hand, concepts revolve around meaning (Seefeldt 2001). Concepts are ideas or basic understandings, within a discipline, that result after analyzing data from a number of experiences. Concepts build from where the child is and become more refined with time and experience. As children's brains develop, so do their concepts of the world, moving from the concrete (plant, flower, insect, roots) to the abstract (growth, beauty, care, cooperation), from the general (plant) to the specific (marigold, impatiens, rose, strawflower). The creation of the associations necessary for children to refine their thoughts over time results in more intellectual development than simple memorization of facts ever could.

In order for children to gain understanding while investigating gardening, you should have a clear idea of what concepts are involved. To clarify this in our own minds, one of the first tasks we undertook in beginning our garden project was the development of a concept web.

### Creating a Concept Web

One way to explore the concepts involved in gardening and to help you think about directions that your garden investigation might take is to create a concept web. This is a way of organizing on paper key ideas to be investigated (Katz and Chard 1993). It provides a visual map of the learning that could occur throughout the project. The process, defined in detail below, often helps teachers to become clear about their own prior knowledge and areas where they might need to access available reference material. Whether or not the children are actually involved in the process of creating the concept web depends on your experience and comfort with webbing, as well as the age group of the children involved. Our concept web on gardening was originally brainstormed by a group of team teachers, with both children and adults adding to it over the life of the project.

Follow this simple five-step procedure for creating a topic web (Katz and Chard, 1993):

1 Cut several small slips of paper or use the smallest size of self-adhesive notes (about 1 by 2 inches). On each slip of paper, write one idea or word that comes to mind when you think of the topic—in this case, gardening. As you brainstorm, write down every word that comes to mind without editing your thoughts. Continue jotting words or ideas, each on a separate slip of paper, until your thoughts on the topic are exhausted. This could take around five to ten minutes, depending on the depth of the topic and your current awareness.

2 Arrange the slips of paper into piles of similar words on a large table or on the floor. If you are working with other teachers or parents, take turns reading these word slips aloud, sorting as you read. Throw out duplicate slips. Try to group words into categories (such as gardening tools or parts of a plant). Place similar groups next to one another. Add new words or ideas, as they come to you, to complete each list.

**3** Create a label or heading which describes each category of ideas. If one group of words is very large, separate it into smaller groups using subheadings.

**4** Focus on digging deeper into this one subject rather than straying too far away from the topic. Some negotiation may be required among the group as categories are finalized. Resource books may be consulted to ensure accurate spelling of terms and correct use of scientific concepts.

**5** Transfer the ideas onto a large poster, which can be displayed in the classroom as a record of the project. Start by placing the general topic—gardening—in the center of the poster. Write out the various lists under their corresponding headings, starting at the outside edge of the paper each time. Sometimes lines or radials are drawn from each of the groups back to the general topic. We have printed our completed garden web as an example, but we recommend that you create your own web based on your personal knowledge, past experience, and regional factors.

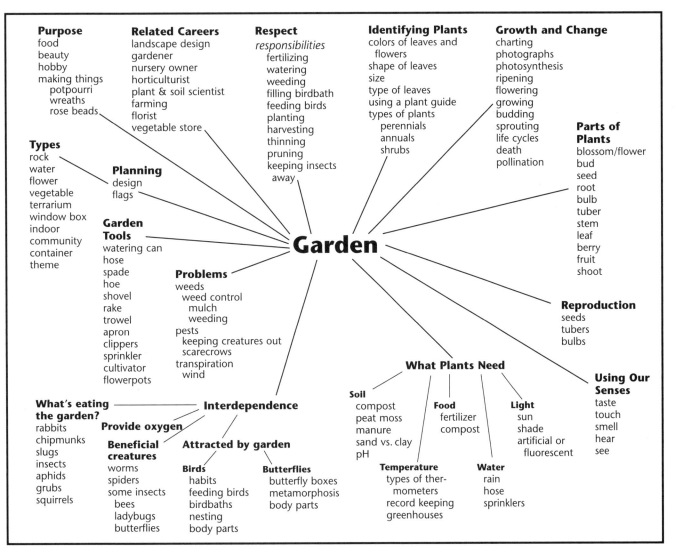

*Created by Sara Starbuck and Marla DeWerff Olthof 1996*

Remember, the topic of gardening can be narrowed down and a web focusing on a single aspect of the garden, such as bugs, flowers, creatures that visit the garden, seeds, vegetables, and so forth, can be created. In fact, the best projects often focus narrowly and intensely on one specific topic. An example of a web on "bugs" can be found in *Young Investigators: The Project Approach in the Early Years* (Helm and Katz 2001, 18). You could narrow the topic further by studying one type of "bug," such as butterflies or ladybugs. Remember, the web serves as a map, keeping you aware of the possible destinations and what awaits you if you decide to go there. You won't necessarily cover every topic on your web. The children's interests should be your guide.

After completing the web, think about how the concepts could be stated in simple terms by the children. Some examples of concepts follow:

- Plants are living things.
- Plants need water to live.
- Some insects eat plants.
- Weeds are plants that we do not want in our garden.

Older children or children who have had more experience with gardening will begin to refine the concepts they are learning and come up with more detailed information:

- Some plants become dormant in the winter and come out of dormancy in the spring.
- Different kinds of plants need different amounts of water to live.
- Some insects eat the insects that eat plants.
- Weeds take the nutrients that other plants need to grow.

Once you are able to state clearly the concepts the child is learning, it becomes easier to evaluate activities for quality.

### Using the Web to Document the Life of the Project

Throughout the life of your garden project, you will want to track the breadth of your study by taking note of the concepts you have covered, as well as the concepts that did not seem to interest the children. One very concrete way of doing this involves posting and using your concept web on a continuous basis. Our concept web and related posters were placed in highly visible areas of the classroom to catch the parents' attention. Creating awareness and enthusiasm in this way not only assisted us in our everyday planning, but also led to a level of parent involvement that we could not have predicted.

We started by placing a check mark next to a concept on the web each time we planned an experience through which it could be explored. Once the planned activity was implemented with the children, we'd circle that check mark on the web. This allowed us to track which concepts were actually being covered by the planned activities.

For example, as we prepared to install our very first plants, we hoped that children would gain a better understanding of concepts such as planting, garden design, the use of flags to specify plant placement, safe handling of garden trowels, and placing roots beneath the soil. After our first day of planting, we met with staff and volunteers to discuss the planning experience. Finally, we circled the check marks next to the concepts we felt were effectively communicated to the children. Looking at the web, you will notice that we did not circle the check mark next to the concept "flags." Our first planting day was fairly chaotic and many of the flags, indicating where certain plants should have been placed, were never installed. We did not use the circle because we did not provide a clear learning experience for the concept.

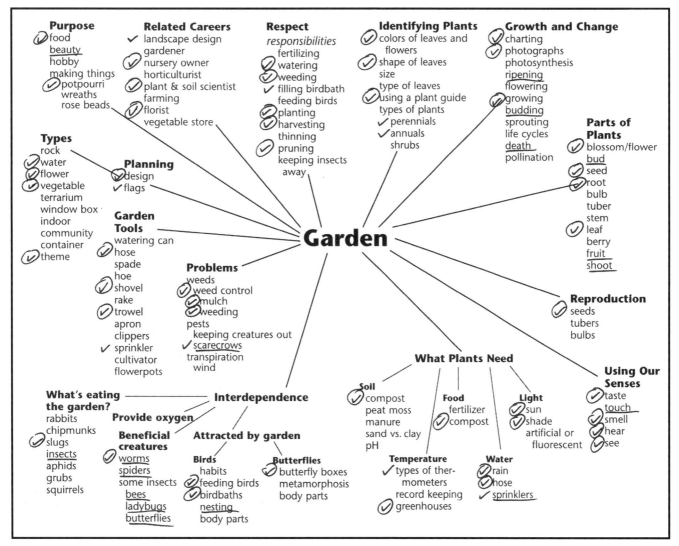

**Purpose**
- food
- beauty
- hobby
- making things
- potpourri
- wreaths
- rose beads

**Related Careers**
- ✓ landscape design
- gardener
- nursery owner
- horticulturist
- plant & soil scientist
- farming
- florist
- vegetable store

**Respect**
*responsibilities*
- fertilizing
- watering
- weeding
- ✓ filling birdbath
- feeding birds
- planting
- harvesting
- thinning
- pruning
- keeping insects away

**Identifying Plants**
- colors of leaves and flowers
- shape of leaves
- size
- type of leaves
- using a plant guide
- types of plants
- ✓ perennials
- ✓ annuals
- shrubs

**Growth and Change**
- charting
- photographs
- photosynthesis
- ripening
- flowering
- growing
- budding
- sprouting
- life cycles
- death
- pollination

**Parts of Plants**
- blossom/flower
- bud
- seed
- root
- bulb
- tuber
- stem
- leaf
- berry
- fruit
- shoot

**Types**
- rock
- water
- flower
- vegetable
- terrarium
- window box
- indoor
- community
- container
- theme

**Planning**
- design
- ✓ flags

**Garden Tools**
- watering can
- hose
- spade
- hoe
- shovel
- rake
- trowel
- apron
- clippers
- ✓ sprinkler
- cultivator
- flowerpots

**Problems**
- weeds
- weed control
- mulch
- weeding
- pests
- keeping creatures out
- ✓ scarecrows
- transpiration
- wind

**Garden**

**Reproduction**
- seeds
- tubers
- bulbs

**What's eating the garden?**
- rabbits
- chipmunks
- slugs
- insects
- aphids
- grubs
- squirrels

**Interdependence**

**Provide oxygen**

**Beneficial creatures**
- worms
- spiders
- some insects
- bees
- ladybugs
- butterflies

**Attracted by garden**

**Birds**
- habits
- feeding birds
- birdbaths
- nesting
- body parts

**Butterflies**
- butterfly boxes
- metamorphosis
- body parts

**What Plants Need**

**Soil**
- compost
- peat moss
- manure
- sand vs. clay
- pH

**Food**
- fertilizer
- compost

**Light**
- sun
- shade
- artificial or fluorescent

**Temperature**
- ✓ types of thermometers
- record keeping
- greenhouses

**Water**
- rain
- hose
- ✓ sprinklers

**Using Our Senses**
- taste
- touch
- smell
- hear
- see

*Created by Sara Starbuck and Marla DeWerff Olthof 1996*

Check marks not circled on the web also indicate times when the children did not show interest or fully engage in the planned activity. For example, an activity based on building a scarecrow for the garden did not interest the children when initially presented. This will happen, especially when working with very young children. Their interests change quickly, and they should not be forced to participate in all planned experiences. Once our flourishing plants and vegetables started to show signs of pest invasion, the children remembered the idea of the scarecrow and it was quickly erected. Seasoned teachers will watch for these teachable moments and use them to address key concepts at a later time.

In fact, careful observation of the children should lead your curriculum. By thoughtfully watching the children as they play, work in the garden, and interact with materials, you will be able to determine what direction you should go in your curriculum planning. By following the children's interests, you can use your web as a road map. By responding to the children, you will keep them eager and involved. To assist us in "mapping" our progress, we underlined the concepts on the web that arose spontaneously through the children's observations and explorations. For instance, when the children noticed anthills on the playground, examined them, and then drew sketches of them in the journal, we underlined "insects" on the web.

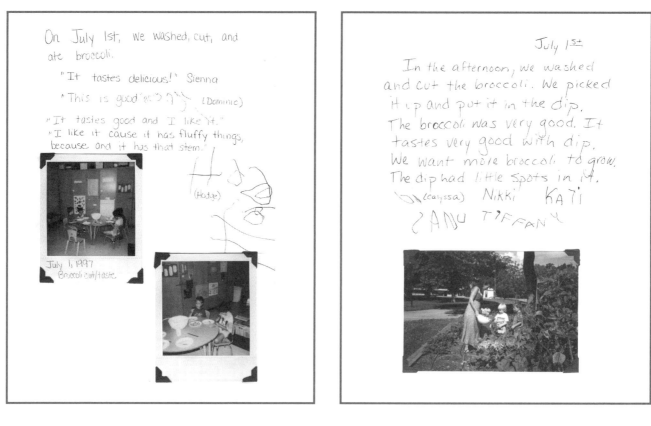

On July 1st, we washed, cut, and ate broccoli.

"It tastes delicious!" Sienna

"This is good as ???" (Dominic)

"It tastes good and I like it."
"I like it cause it has fluffy things, because and it has that stem."

(Hodge)

July 1, 1997
Broccoli cut/taste.

July 1st

In the afternoon, we washed and cut the broccoli. We picked it up and put it in the dip. The broccoli was very good. It tastes very good with dip. We want more broccoli to grow. The dip had little spots in it.
(Calyssa) Nikki KATI
?ANU TIFFANY

These techniques provided a clear picture of what information had been covered and where we could go with future planning. We relied on our web during staff meetings to provide a framework for planning and lend a forward motion to our project. Visiting parents enjoyed checking the web regularly, as well, to track the group's learning about the garden.

Not every concept on the web needs to be addressed in one project. The topic of gardening provides endless learning opportunities that will continue over a lifetime. The children's learning will be built upon year by year, experience by experience. Some concepts, such as planting, weeding, and watering, are universal, while the related careers and purposes for gardening that you study will vary by region, culture, and age of the group. Rather than feeling pressured to investigate every concept, we recommend you try to follow the interests of individuals or small groups as they develop.

## Integrating the Curriculum

Young children are integrated beings. Their physical development affects their cognitive development, which affects the development of language, which affects social development. As teachers who work with young children, we know that we can't divide a child up, dealing first with one part and then another. Instead, we focus on the child's overall development by integrating activities to address the whole child. By focusing on a topic, such as gardening, and carefully designing activities that address many curricular areas, we help children build conceptual development and deeper understanding (Bredekamp and Rosegrant 1992).

Consider a typical activity in which children might participate during a garden project: making individual pizzas from English muffins with green peppers and tomatoes from the garden. As they follow the recipe, the children are exposed to literacy. They talk and, with the help of the teacher, are exposed to new vocabulary words. They work on social skills as they take turns and negotiate tasks. The children use fine motor skills in cutting the vegetables and preparing the pizzas. They participate in math as they classify, count, and divide the vegetables into pieces. They divide the English muffins in half and are exposed to fractions. They count the number of pizzas they are making and experience one-to-one correspondence as they place ingredients on each English muffin half. The children have observed scientific processes as they watched the changes in the tomatoes and peppers growing in the garden. Now they will see the insides of the vegetables and notice the seeds (basic biology). They will watch the changes that occur in the pizzas as they are heated (changes in state—physics). Later, they will record their experience in their journal (more literacy). One could go on and on. Rich classroom experiences bring many disciplines together.

A garden project is full of opportunities to integrate the curriculum. Every aspect of the curriculum can be woven into a project on gardening, and a wise teacher plans ahead to include each discipline within the activities planned for the child.

Be cautious, however, not to focus solely on gardening. Many teachers remember experiences in their schooling when they were expected to plan units revolving around a specific

theme. Sometimes the expectation was that every planned activity would be based on this theme. So teachers struggled to come up with art activities on insects or fine motor activities that involved pets. Some teachers still do this. The result of this kind of planning, however, is often contrived activities that have little meaning to the children and that lack intellectual integrity. To avoid this trap, plan several strong activities related to gardening. Then plan other activities that are simply good activities involving basic materials and equipment, not necessarily connected to the garden. If you feel like you are straining too hard to come up with a certain kind of garden-related activity, you probably need to pull back. Remember, if you have to stretch to make a connection, the children probably won't get it.

As you proceed with your garden project, you'll want to be sure that you are integrating all the disciplines into the gardening experience. This book is designed to enable you to create a rich curriculum for children by responding to their interests and following their lead. Periodically take the time to review your project to ensure that your in-depth study of the garden provides a breadth of experiences.

## Asking Questions

Questions have the ability to provoke thought, to challenge perceptions, to invite reflection, to spur action. They are important if children are to reach beyond the obvious in their explorations and make new discoveries. A disposition to question is essential to a lifelong learner

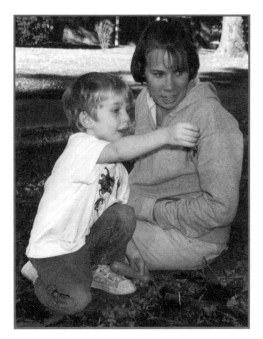

and one attribute common among people who rise to greatness. Teachers need to be able to model questioning in order to build this disposition in children. They also need to ask questions to encourage children to think and evaluate, to look beyond the obvious, to stretch their minds.

But questions also have the capacity to stop children in their tracks, to impede learning, to discourage. Think of a social situation where you were uncomfortable and trying to involve someone in conversation. If you asked a simple yes-or-no question, it probably received a quick answer. The same may be true if you asked a question with only one correct answer. Unless you are dealing with someone who enjoys talking or you hit upon a subject in which the other person is very interested, you may find that such questions actually stop conversation. Watch a talented interviewer on television. She carefully constructs questions that will cause the person being interviewed to share, reflect, and expand on thoughts. Likewise, good teachers give ample thought before posing questions to children.

First, consider whether a question is convergent or divergent. Convergent questions, sometimes referred to as "closed" questions, have a single, correct answer. They can help focus children's attention and can be useful at the beginning of a conversation: "Which plant is taller, the sunflower or the marigold?" Or they can help children recall prior events: "What was the first thing that happened to the seed after we put it in the soil?" However, you must be cautious not to ask convergent questions just for the sake of hearing answers. You should not stop after asking a convergent question, but continue to encourage the child to extract meaning from the experience and seek out new experiences that expand on learning. If the child is to be challenged to learn and to think creatively, the teacher must follow convergent questions with divergent questions.

Divergent questions, often called "open-ended" questions, can have many answers. They encourage children to consider what has happened, explore further, examine relationships, and discover answers for themselves: "Why do you think there are holes in the leaf?" or, "How could we stop the aphids from eating our plants?"

In *Science with Young Children* (1989), Holt examines and evaluates eight types of questions teachers ask. Holt concludes, "Questions are best and most successfully used to start discussion if the teacher does not already know the answer, if there is no generally correct answer, or if the question asks for the opinions and experiences of each person as her own authority." She suggests that if teachers want to test children to find out if they know something, they be honest and tell the child this before proceeding with the question, and that if they have information they want to share with the child, that they simply tell them. By following these guidelines, teachers develop honest relationships with children that will serve them well as they become partners in investigating and learning.

# Types of Questions Teachers Ask

| Type of Question | Who Knows the Answer | Advantages | Disadvantages |
|---|---|---|---|
| One correct answer | Almost everyone | Few advantages | Risks insulting the children. ("Does the teacher think I'm stupid?") |
| One correct answer | Teacher knows, is virtually certain children do not | Few advantages | Not very sensible. Why would someone who knows the answer ask those who do not? Discourages reverence for questioning attitude. |
| One correct answer | Children know, teacher does not | Legitimate request for information; recognition that children have information teacher needs | Beware of using as a means of enforcing limits. ("Who left their coat on the floor?) |
| One correct answer | Teacher knows, some children know and some do not | Good for beginning discussion or responding to child's response with another question | Teacher should be careful not to dominate conversation; encourage children to talk to one another |
| Any question | No one present knows, but the teacher thinks he does | No advantage | Children are exposed to inaccurate or misleading information |
| No correct answer | No one knows, and people know this | Communicates respect for unknowns | Can lead to misinformation if teacher is unwilling to admit she doesn't know |
| Probably has a correct answer | No one present | Can lead in a search for correct answers through research or experimentation | None |
| Many correct answers | Each person has own answer | Great for starting discussions | None |

*Source: Adapted from: Holt, Bess-Gene (1989)*

Isenberg and Jalongo (2001, 420) recommend including thinking words in questions. For instance, instead of asking, "What do you think will happen if . . . ?" the teacher would ask, "What do you *predict* will happen if . . . ?" This technique gives children a beginning understanding of the scientific process and shows that you take their investigations seriously.

Harlan and Rivkin (1996) describe seven types of divergent questions. The following chart shows examples of how these can be adapted to gardening.

## Seven Types of Divergent Questions

| Purpose of Question | Examples |
|---|---|
| Instigating discovery | What kind of environment do earthworms prefer? How do the leaves of different flowers look different? Why are there holes in the leaves of our beans? Why is the tomato lying on the ground with a bite out of it? |
| Eliciting predictions | What do you predict will happen if we don't water this plant? What do you predict will happen if we plant the sunflower in the shade? |
| Probing for understanding | Why do you think this marigold is taller than that marigold? Why do you think that plant died? |
| Promoting reasoning | Why do you think the worms crawled under the damp paper towel? What evidence do you have to support that? What conclusions can you draw from that? |
| Serving as a catalyst | What could we do to keep the birds from eating the berries? What could we do to keep the soil from drying out so quickly? |
| Encouraging creative thinking | What would happen if the stores quit selling vegetables? What would happen if plants never stopped growing? |
| Reflecting on feelings | What was it like sitting alone inside the sunflower house? How did you feel when you found the big pumpkin in the garden? What was the best part of watching the ants working in the garden? |

## Using Reference Materials

A large part of your job as a teacher involves pointing children in the right direction when they have a question. To assist children in this endeavor, you need to be sure that you have reference materials available, so that children can find the answers they seek. Some children will naturally think to check reference materials for added information, while others might need your prompting to seek out these resources. Consulting with books, encyclopedias, seed catalogs, gardening magazines, CD-ROMs, videos, and the Internet provides children with factual information and often leads to further scientific research.

When our children noticed the hostas were badly eaten, they pointed out the problem to Sara. She helped them to observe and identify slugs as the guilty culprits. Together they consulted one of the many gardening books on the shelf to read about slugs and get ideas for what to do next. They decided to try a recipe for slug repellent that required yeast, water, and sugar. The children followed the recipe and attempted to save the hostas. They wrote about this experience in the garden journal and observed for the next several days to see if it worked. This experience taught these preschoolers the value of nonfiction reference materials and an important lesson on the benefits of literacy.

### Journal entry from July 1996

The children made a slug trap to try to catch the slugs that were eating our hostas. This is their dictation:

"We made a slug trap in the dinosaur garden so they wouldn't bite our plants. We got some water and yeast and sugar. We put them in a bowl and we digged so it would fit in. We hope we catch some slugs. They will drown. The slugs will drown. No more Mr. Slug. And no more Mrs. Slug. And no more baby slug. And no Grandpa or Grandma slugs. And no friend slugs."

## References

Bredekamp, Sue, and Teresa Rosegrant, eds. 1992. *Reaching potentials: Appropriate curriculum and assessment for young children*, vol. 1. Washington, D.C.: NAEYC.

Chard, Sylvia. 1998. *The project approach: Making curriculum come alive*. New York: Scholastic.

Cornell, Joseph. 1979. *Sharing nature with children*. Nevada City, Calif.: Dawn Publications.

Harlan, Jean D., and Mary S. Rivkin. 1996. *Science experiences for the early childhood years*. Englewood Cliffs, N.J.: Prentice-Hall, Inc.

Helm, Judy Harris, and Lilian G. Katz. 2001. *Young investigators: The project approach in the early years*. New York: Teachers College Press.

Holt, Bess-Gene. 1989. *Science with young children*. Washington, D.C.: NAEYC.

Isenberg, Joan Packer, and Mary Renck Jalongo. 2001. *Creative expression and play in early childhood*. Upper Saddle River, N.J.: Merrill Prentice Hall, Inc.

Katz, Lilian G. 1993. Dispositions: Definitions and implications for early childhood practice. *ERIC/EECE Publications* Catalog # 211: April 1993.

———. 1994. *The project approach*. Champaign, Ill.: ERIC Clearinghouse on Elementary and Early Childhood Education.

Katz, Lilian G., and Sylvia C. Chard. 1993. *Engaging children's minds: The project approach*. Norwood, N.J.: Ablex Publishing Corporation.

Lowenstein, Frank, and Sheryl Lechner. 1999. *Bugs: Insects, spiders, centipedes, millipedes, and other closely related arthropods*. New York: Black Dog and Leventhal Publishers, Inc.

Seefeldt, Carol. 2001. *Social studies for the preschool-primary child*. Columbus, Ohio: Merrill Prentice Hall.

# 2

# Engaging Children
in Gardening

Successful projects engage children mentally, physically, and emotionally. To do this, a gardening project must have an on-site garden at its core. Children must feel ownership through the acts of planning, planting, tending, observing, and exploring. Any gardening project that does not involve children in these types of activities will be short-lived at best. As the proverb says, "I hear, I forget. I see, I remember. I do, I understand." If you want children to learn about gardening, then they must do it on a daily basis for some length of time. They will need repeated experiences to solidify and refine the concepts they learn, such as what a plant

needs to grow. Children need time to become attached to the garden, to treasure it, to study it, to play in it, and to understand how it works. In this chapter, we will describe how to foster personal investment and common knowledge, engage children in the process of discussing what they already know about gardens and what they want to learn, plan fieldwork, choose garden themes, and document children's learning throughout the project.

## Fostering Children's Interest in Gardening

When beginning a project, teachers must first foster children's interest and personal investment in the topic. Your goal here is to create a common background of experience for the class to enrich their discussions and interactions before they begin the act of gardening (Helm and Katz 2001). In the

spring, children are often fascinated by the changes they see in the outdoor world around them. You can capitalize on this natural curiosity by adding books about gardening to your class library. Introduce gardening poems, songs, and storybooks at circle time to initiate discussions of gardening. Hang posters of gardens or flowers around the room, or take a nature walk to look for signs of spring as motivation for children to verbally share their past experiences with plants and gardening. Provide familiar gardening props for dramatic play to help children access memories of garden-related activities and inspire more discussion. Over a period of several days, you will discover which children have prior experience working in gardens or flower-beds. Encourage children to share personal stories at group meeting times. Foster conversations among children throughout the day about previous experience with planting, growing, and harvesting. All of these activities will allow children to recall basic knowledge and vocabulary related to gardening.

## Engaging Children in the K-W-L Process

Once the children have become interested in the topic of plants and gardening, sit down with the children, in either large or small groups, to engage them in a process called "K-W-L." Donna Ogle (1986) designed this strategy to help children with reading comprehension. Here, this strategy is adapted to help children organize their thoughts as they prepare to study a specific topic. With this teaching technique, children are asked to define what they *Know* about a subject, then create a list of questions detailing what they *Want* to know, and finally, summarize what they have *Learned* about the topic.

### Finding Out What Children Know

The first step, *K*, involves making a list of all the facts the children currently *Know* about gardens and gardening. Your goal here is to try to find out what they understand, remember, or have noticed about plants and gardens. Record children's statements on a large chart or poster in sentence form. Do not spend time elaborating on each point the children make, correcting their mistaken ideas, or trying to teach additional information. Those steps are reserved for the second phase. Ogle (1986) suggests that you select key words for this type

of brainstorming that are specific enough to generate important information needed for the project. For example, when preparing for your garden project, ask the children what they know about gardening, not what they know about springtime, or what happens in the springtime. A general discussion of springtime may never allow the group to focus on gardening itself. If the children appear to have little knowledge of gardening, then ask the more general question, "What do you know about plants and seeds?" At this level, the group is sure to have some basic knowledge.

# Group Size and the K-W-L Process

Each stage of the K-W-L process can be completed in either small or large groups. You will need to analyze your teaching situation and group dynamic to decide what group size is best for each step in the process. Both group sizes have advantages and disadvantages. Large groups are effective when

- the teacher-child ratios are high
- the children are in the habit of meeting in a large group
- the age group is mixed
- you want to foster a sense of community among the group

Meanwhile, small groups tend to work better when

- the teacher-child ratios are at a minimum
- the children within the group have diverse attention spans or levels of development
- the topic of discussion is very focused and only of interest to specific children

If you are working in a preschool program with a high teacher-to-child ratio, with at least one teacher to every seven or eight children, you should be able to use large group times effectively throughout the life of a project. When children meet daily to hold a circle time or large group meeting, the process is simplified. If you hold regular meetings, you will usually have students who understand the social expectations of the situation, such as waiting a turn to talk and addressing the whole group when speaking. If you are in a preschool classroom serving a mixed-age group, large group times can provide an opportunity for older children to model for younger students in the areas of communication skills, attention span, and question formation.

The effective use of large group discussions with young children takes considerable practice and skill. Yet large group discussion fosters a sense of community and facilitates shared decision making, creating "cross-child communication," in which you encourage the children to respond and make suggestions to each other (Helm and Katz 2001). This type of interaction is very different from the ping-pong type of interaction we might typically see in large group scenarios, where you pose a question and each child in turn responds and is acknowledged by you, until everyone has a turn. Skilled teachers will invite the group to consider and respond to each child's contribution to the discussion at hand.

Nevertheless, you should not be surprised or discouraged if some children seem restless during large group discussions. This is normal for young children. One way to handle this challenge is to hold the discussion near the end of circle time, perhaps during the last five minutes. This way, children whose attention is diverted can be dismissed gradually to the next step in the daily routine, such as free choice time or snack. This allows children who are fully engaged to focus and communicate with fewer distractions.

Small group discussions, on the other hand, may work best in classrooms where the teacher-child ratio is minimal, such as one teacher to every ten children. Teachers in this situation may prefer to meet with children in smaller groups during free play time, both indoors and out. The use of small groups also allows you to meet the varying attention spans and developmental levels of children within the group, since children can move freely in and out of these groups without disrupting the flow of ideas. The small group format also lends itself well to detailed discussion of specific aspects of a topic, which may be of high interest to some children but of no interest to others. Forcing children who are not interested in the discussion to take part in it creates unnecessary power struggles and guidance issues. Small group interactions support developmentally appropriate practice because they give children the choice to be fully engaged by the current topic of discussion, or to move to a more personally stimulating activity.

At this point, you may uncover some misinformation that children have, which will need to be clarified through hands-on gardening and consistent use of the scientific process. As a facilitator of group discussion, you will want to make a mental note of areas where children offer conflicting information or where they seem to lack confidence in the validity of their statements. This information will be useful to you later as you plan learning activities for groups and individual students.

## Planning Based on What Children Want to Learn

At this point you are ready to reflect on what the children know, as well as what you know about gardening, which should be outlined in the form of a concept web (see chapter 1). Using  this information, you can begin to plan activities and experiences for the group. Each word or phrase on the web now represents a concept to be explored. We suggest planning some initial activities and then observing and documenting children's interests, letting them guide you in selecting the next concepts to be explored. In *Bringing Reggio Emilia Home* (1997), Louise Cadwell compares this responsive teaching style to the exchange of a ball on a court or playing field. Sometimes teachers have the ball as they set up the environment, lead discussions with stimulating questions, and provide exposure to new tools or techniques. At other times, the ball is passed to the children, who steer the project in a certain direction by providing input and using shared decision making.

One way to pass the ball to children when planning is to engage in the *W* step of the K-W-L process described earlier. Talk to children in large or small groups to find out what they *Want* to know about gardening. It helps to quickly review the poster made earlier highlighting what they already *Know*. Then ask the group, "What do you want to know about gardens or gardening?" Write down their questions word for word, just as they phrase them. Jones and Nimmo (1995), authors of *Emergent Curriculum*, suggest thinking of the teacher's role as that of scribe, rather than editor, during these dictation sessions to show respect for children's growing language abilities. You can write the children's names after their specific questions if you wish, in order to  follow up during later discussions. For instance, you might later prompt, "Jeremy, remember last week when you wanted to know about what plants eat? Well, today in the book area, we have a book that might help you answer that question. Would you like to read it with me at work time?"

You may change to more general terms if you get no response, "What do you want to know about plants?" Younger children, or children engaging in this process for the first time, will need a lot of teacher support through this process. You may need to reformulate their statements into questions such as, "So are you saying, John, that you want to know why bumblebees like to buzz around flowers?"

We have also found that we sometimes need to model question formation for a group that has difficulty getting started. We learned to do this by adapting the reading instruction strategy of Beth Davey (1983), which she calls "think-aloud." When children have difficulty forming their own questions and the discussion is stalled, you might say something such as, "Well, I have always wondered if there are any plants that will grow in the shade. Has anyone else ever wondered about that? Do you think we should write that down as something we'd like to learn as we garden?" If children respond positively, write the question on the chart and then ask the children, "What else do you want to know? Who else has a question?" This modeling should provide a sense of framework to the task and get the group going.

This is a good time to recall aloud, or read from the original poster, those areas of disagreement or doubt from the first group discussion on what the children already knew about gardening. Encourage children to share different viewpoints on the topic and assist children in formulating these issues into questions to be investigated. Remember to be sensitive to the fact that some children will not feel comfortable speaking in front of the group. Tell the group that questions can and will be added to the list as the project moves forward. Post the list where children can reach it and invite them to handwrite or dictate additional questions during work time.

## Documenting What Children Learn

As you explore gardening you will want to document the journey the children take in their understanding. Documenting simply means to record, analyze, interpret, and display what children have *Learned* about gardening. This brings us to the third step of the K-W-L process. The children need to investigate their questions, find answers, and represent their learning over and over again to personalize and solidify learning. Children represent what they know about a subject through speaking, singing, writing, drawing, building, and acting out scenarios. Teachers need to find ways to record this process for use in further planning and conveying information about specific children to parents and administrators. There are so many approaches to documentation of young children's learning that we could not describe them all in this book. For a complete description of documentation methods in early childhood we suggest the book *Windows on Learning: Documenting Young Children's Work* (Helm, Beneke, and Steinheimer 1998). Here, we will discuss the two techniques we used most frequently during our years of gardening with children: journals and storyboards. Remember that the web discussed in chapter 1 and the fieldwork follow-up techniques described later in this chapter also fall into the category of documentation.

### *Journals*

Keeping a garden journal over the life of a project has many benefits. Children learn to apply emergent literacy and numeracy skills, as well as the benefits of recording scientific data. They learn that their thoughts, feelings, observations, and experiments can be recorded in various forms and interpreted by others.

Journaling can occur in two formats, either as a group or individually. With preschoolers, we experienced a great deal of success using the group journal format. The first two

On April 15, 1997, we took a trip to the greenhouse and saw...

"This was soil for the plants." - Neil

"When Nyssa's mom was talking about the flowers." - Hodge

6·20·00

Sara, Kit, Tyler, and Lisa planted Marigold's. Kit worked on her own and Tyler helped Lisa. Sara also worked on her own, but helped Kit, Tyler and Lisa too. Kit also dug for worms.

years, we bought a hardcover, spiral-bound sketchbook with blank pages. This allowed children the freedom to draw, create graphs, mount photos, or write stories. Our portable playground shed provided a safe, but accessible, storage place so children could record spontaneous observations, as well as teacher-planned activities. Using only one journal allowed us to compare the interests of the morning and afternoon groups, as well as observe the overall progress of the project. Unfortunately, it also meant that two children or two small groups could not use the book at one time. Therefore, our third year, we changed to a page-by-page scrapbook format. A few pages were kept in the playground shed, while a few were kept within children's reach in the classroom. Finished pages were periodically reviewed and added to the journal. This system allowed several children and adults to record information and document garden-related activities simultaneously. Both of these group journal formats fostered a sense of community among the group.

Kindergarten students can keep individual garden journals if given the time and motivation to do so. The teacher plays a critical role here, holding weekly meetings with each student about the journal, providing opportunities for children to explain journal entries to others, and adding challenge as necessary to build developing skills. Some children will eagerly write or draw each day, while others will need to be reminded. Some children need structured assignments, while others perform better with less structure. Louise Boyd Cadwell (1997, 124) writes about a kindergarten class that planted bean seeds and kept Bean Journals. Each child was invited to draw, write, and record measurements of a specific bean plant as it grew. This project lasted sixty to seventy days, as children fine-tuned their observation, documentation, and representation skills.

While some common elements will emerge in all journals, no two journals will be exactly the same. A successful journal will provide detailed documentation such as

- dates
- descriptions of major scientific processes
- experiment predictions and outcomes
- key vocabulary words
- observations
- charts and graphs
- photographs at key stages
- poems and songs
- short stories
- favorite recipes
- children's dictation
- children's artwork

Whatever your combination of the above, journaling will help children remember what happened at various stages, understand the strategies used by people for remembering information, learn from past experiences, and plan for the future.

## Storyboards

A good way for teachers to share what is happening in the classroom with parents and other visitors is through story or documentation boards. These exhibits include photographs of the children engaged in play or exploration, along with a written story of what happened. We also include a statement about how the activity relates to the children's learning and development. This statement provides an educational purpose in showing adults the value of play. For a detailed description of how to make storyboards, see *The Art of Awareness* (Curtis and Carter 2000). Our storyboard about sprouting seeds is on the next page.

Storyboards have many uses. We post ours in our large lobby area so that the parents can see what the children in different classes are doing. Here, they are also viewed by visitors and prospective parents. Parents often stop with their children and read the boards together. Sometimes we also display the boards outside the center to show the community what we're doing.

Storyboards can also be displayed in the classroom. Here children will repeatedly refer to them, recalling an activity in which they previously engaged. Sometimes they will be compelled to add to what has been written. As children are exposed to storyboards, they will probably want to make their own. Teachers can take photos for children to use and take dictation for children who are not yet able to write. (Very brave teachers might let children take their own photographs.)

Documentation of the knowledge, skills, and dispositions developed while gardening is important at all stages of the project. Careful planning will allow you to capture the children's basic awareness at the beginning of the project by saving lists of what children initially know and say about gardening. You will value this information as you compare it with the learning documented later in the life of the project.

# Seed Sprouting in the Classroom

We filled the sensory table with potting soil, then added water to the soil until it was moist. We put bean seeds in the soil and left them there for almost two weeks. At first we noticed that the beans were beginning to swell.

The beans soon started to grow roots. The shoots and the roots continued to grow. Every day we checked them and every day they were bigger. The teachers noticed that when the children played in the soil, they carefully dug around the seeds. Few of the sprouts were damaged even though children played in the sensory table every day.

Finally, we decided to plant the seeds in a planting box, so we could grow them outside. The children filled the box with the potting soil, then carefully moved the bean seeds and covered them with soil. We took the planters outside and placed them next to the garden to watch them grow.

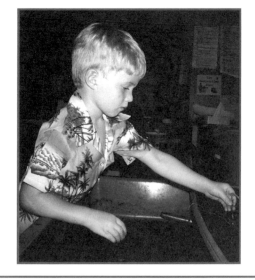

**Learning and Developing:** Through this activity, the children had a rare chance to observe and study the sprouting seeds close up. Usually this event occurs underground, out of sight. Because the bean sprouts were sturdy, the children were able to examine them daily, touching them and feeling the tender sprouts and roots. The children explored actively with all their senses, discovering the relationship of the bean seed to the plant through direct experience. They used language to describe what they were seeing and to share their observations with others.

# Fieldwork

Taking a trip to a special location for the purpose of research enhances any project as children seek answers to questions for which they feel ownership. We refer to these trips as fieldwork, rather than field trips, because the role of the child resembles that of a scientist more than the tourist approach of traditional field trips. The best way to select a site for fieldwork is to get to know your community. Refer back to your concept web and the children's list of questions, then check your local yellow pages for businesses or locations where you might explore the concepts or find answers. Ask parents and coworkers about personal contacts they might have related to your topic.

One of our favorite fieldwork trips related to gardening was arranged by a preschool parent and took place at a local greenhouse. The children first planted seeds in flats at school. The parent then transported the seeds to the greenhouse for early care and sprouting. A few weeks later, we arranged for the children to visit their seedlings and learn more about the greenhouse. The children observed, touched, sniffed, and sketched the plants. They also learned firsthand about the overhead sprinklers. Eventually, those seedlings were brought back to school and planted in our garden. This led to meaningful hands-on gardening and continued personal investment on the part of the children. During our project, smaller walking trips were also taken to various nearby flowerbeds and landscaped areas on the university campus, including a Japanese garden. Other fieldwork sites related to gardening might include the following: the garden tool and fertilizer section of a local discount store, a local nursery, local parks with community gardens, a flower shop, or the home of an avid gardener.

## Before the Trip

Meaningful learning doesn't just happen on a fieldwork trip. You will need to set the stage for maximum learning opportunities. Poor planning on your part might actually lead to situations where children are prevented from noticing and recording the detailed information they will need later in the project. In this section, we will describe how to set the stage by visiting the site in advance, keeping adult-child ratios low, preparing fieldwork backpacks, and creating research teams within your class.

### Visiting the Site in Advance

You can increase learning opportunities by spending a short time visiting the site prior to the actual trip. This will also allow you and the site expert to feel confident and prepared. Remember to consider safety factors in the environment and communicate your research goals to the expert. You will probably need to be very specific with the site expert about the attention span of the age group you are serving. Expecting three-year-olds to listen to a twenty-minute lecture on fertilizer would be as inappropriate as only allowing five minutes for kindergarten students to draw the inner-workings of a greenhouse. Yet, those who do not serve young children on a daily basis may not have this knowledge and will need your professional opinion on such matters.

### Keeping Adult-Child Ratio Low

Another fieldwork strategy involves limiting the number of children who attend at one time or increasing the number of adults, so that children can get a great deal of support while observing, asking questions, and recording data. Always invite parents to volunteer on fieldwork trips

to provide the extra eyes, ears, and hands needed to keep everyone safe and focused. You might also consider hiring extra staff, such as substitutes, on these days to increase the number of adults on the trip. Or ask your supervisor or principal to attend the trip and support the class in doing research. To control the number of children on each trip, we have traditionally split our group of twenty-four preschoolers in two, taking half in the morning, with the other half attending in the afternoon. With preschoolers, this technique works beautifully to ensure that children who nap consistently do not miss fieldwork opportunities. This technique also gives parent volunteers an option to take off half of the day, rather than miss an entire day of work. Your

actual adult-child ratio on these trips will depend on your state laws and on safety factors specific to each fieldwork site.

### Preparing Fieldwork Backpacks

For every trip, you will want to prepare several items to take along. We created a "fieldwork backpack" that was taken on every trip and restocked upon return to school. We went to a local discount store and purchased an adult-sized backpack, such as the ones carried by the college students on our campus. The pack included an 8½-by-11-inch clipboard for each of the four teams. To each clipboard we attached several sheets of blank white paper and a plastic baggy with colored markers or pencils. When selecting writing utensils, remember that children need to write as well as document what they see using a variety of colors. Therefore, a full set of fine-tipped markers or sharpened colored pencils is recommended for each team. When clipboards are well-stocked in this manner, one set of documentation tools can be handed out quickly to each research team upon arrival at the fieldwork site.

The pack also contained a 35mm camera, and extra film for taking photos. In addition, we included emergency items such as medical/contact information sheets for all children, a first aid kit, moist towelettes, and a clean change of clothing for the occasional potty accident. We recommend checking the backpack thoroughly before each trip to make sure that pencils are sharpened, the camera is loaded with film, clipboards are stocked with adequate paper for each team, the change of clothing is seasonally appropriate, and the emergency information is up-to-date.

## Creating Research Teams

When planning fieldwork, you can assign children to specific research teams that balance their developing skills. For example, each team will need one child who can draw, one who has emergent writing skills, and one who is confident enough to ask questions of the site expert. You might arrange for the youngest children, or children with the shortest attention spans, to have their own team. This way, special activities can be planned for them while the other groups continue their research. Once, on a trip to a local nursery and garden store, we arranged a scavenger hunt for the three-year-olds while the older children sketched and printed the names of their favorite plants. The teacher visited the site ahead of time and made a list of objects for the three-year-olds to find, such as a red flower, a frog statue, and a wind sock. This activity helped time pass quickly for both children and adults, while allowing detailed research and data collection to continue.

Within your defined research teams, children will meet regularly prior to the trip to talk about what they might see, divide responsibilities, and brainstorm specific research questions on which to focus. In essence, you will repeat the K-W-L process in each of these small groups. This time the children will be describing what they know about the site and what happens there. In a second small group session, each team should make a list of research questions to be answered by careful observation or by interviewing the site expert. One trick that we find useful is to write or type each child's research questions on a computer address label, along with her name. On the day of the trip, stick these to the children's shirts or jackets so volunteers know the children's names and can remind them of their questions. This technique helps each team to focus on collecting specific data. Another idea is to type each team's list of questions and distribute these to the parents and volunteers who attend. You might even want to forward these lists to the site expert a day or two before the trip so she can be sure to highlight these issues during the visit.

## During the Trip

During the fieldwork trip, challenge children to listen to the site expert and look closely at the environment while thinking about their specific research questions. Be sure to allow plenty of time for each group to ask questions, record answers, or draw on their clipboards. Encourage parents to write their own notes and take dictation from children about drawings and sketches. Take plenty of photos, especially of the plants, equipment, and structures that the children attempt to draw. This will allow children to add details to drawings in the days ahead. If a portable video camera is available, document the trip in this manner. Try to circulate among each

research team and videotape at least a portion of the events or objects most clearly related to their research questions.

If site experts use terminology that is beyond the understanding of your group, ask them to say it another way or explain it in more detail. If necessary, take it upon yourself to adapt the words of the site expert to a level your group can comprehend and record. Remember to use the think-aloud technique discussed earlier to help children compare what they hear or see on the trip to their previous knowledge. For example, you might say, "If these plants like to grow in shade, then they might like to grow at our school in the shade behind the shed or under the big oak tree." As you return to school, remind everyone to turn in or save all field notes (sketches, written data, samples) collected during the trip for further follow-up study.

## After the Trip

The day after the trip you will want to meet with each research team to assist them in reviewing their field notes, watching video clips, drawing conclusions, and formulating new questions. At this time, you can also help the group decide on a way to represent and share with others what they *Learned* on the field trip. This brings the K-W-L process full circle. There are many formats for representing what children have learned to the rest of the class. Answers to questions can be printed on the class computer and distributed as handouts to accompany an oral presentation to parents. When children refer to photos and video taken on the trip, their sketches can be refined, labeled in detail, and mounted on cardboard for display. Sketches can also be photocopied onto transparencies and projected onto the wall. The projected images are then traced on large paper and colored or painted as a mural (Helm and Katz 2001).

Photos can be used in a homemade book, bulletin board, or even a narrated slide show. Summarizing children's learning through a narrated slide show requires careful preparation. First, 35mm photos will need to be made into slides if special slide film was not used. Or these

photos could be scanned into a computer and projected onto a screen in a multimedia presentation. A third option is to use a digital camera to create a computerized slide show. Also, since some children will freeze in front of the group and forget what they were going to say, it is best to pretape their narration by meeting with the team privately in advance. We had great success with this strategy. Each photo was numbered. Then each photo was shown to the children and a question was posed about the photo, such as, "What do you remember about this photo?" or, "What do you see in this photo?" Then a tape recorder was used to record the children's responses one at a time about each photo. Again, it is sometimes necessary to remind children of what they saw on the trip just prior to making this tape by reviewing with them your notes or their sketches. Class time for making these types of presentations should be arranged and scheduled so that parents, administrators, or other classes can be invited to attend. We found circle time to be an appropriate venue for this type of sharing in our preschool classroom.

In the process of helping children to represent their learning, some teachers find that children are missing key pieces of information. This sometimes sparks a return trip to the fieldwork site the following week. The entire group can visit the site if it is within walking distance of the school or if transportation is readily available. If this is not feasible, the teacher or a parent can return to the site to take additional video or photographs to use in rounding out children's observations, sketches, and research findings, or answering new questions that have developed.

## Graphing with Children

Graphs can provide an effective way to collect and record data and also serve as useful tools in solving problems and making decisions related to gardening. A garden project offers many opportunities to involve children with graphing in meaningful ways. It's best to start with what Baratta-Lorton (1976) calls "real graphs." These graphs use actual objects such as people or vegetables to form the graph. The use of real graphs forms the foundation for other, more abstract, graphing activities.

Opportunities to create real graphs can be planned. For example, a real graph using people might answer the question, "Which garden job would you like to do this week—watering or mulching?" To answer this question, you would post two pictures on the wall or floor, one of someone watering and one of someone mulching. Then the children would select the task they want to do by standing in one of the two lines. You can make this experience even less abstract by using real objects rather than pictures to identify the lines. For example you can say, "If you watered the garden this week, please line up behind this watering can."

Once children are in their lines, you should help them count aloud the number of children in each line. Then you can ask a series of questions, such as

- How many children want to water the garden?
- How many want to mulch?
- Which line has the most children—watering or mulching?
- Which line has the fewest children?
- How many more (or fewer) children watered than mulched?

Children with experience using people graphs will eventually be able to choose between three options, such as watering, mulching, or weeding.

After much practice with real graphs, the children should be shown how to record this information in the form of a picture graph. For the above example, you would give each child a small photocopied or computer-printed picture of someone either watering or mulching, depending on which line he is in. These pictures would then be taped to a graph that was prepared in advance. You would then ask the same series of questions as above.

Real graphs can also be completed using three-dimensional objects, such as fruits and vegetables. For example, you might say, "Today we picked cherry tomatoes and green beans. Are there more tomatoes or more green beans?" The children would then create a line of cherry tomatoes next to a line of green beans. With this type of activity, it is sometimes helpful to have a blank laminated graph with evenly-spaced squares to make comparison easier. Then one bean or one tomato would be placed in each square.

Ideas that are repeated many times in various ways have the most impact on children's learning. Real graphs should be used repeatedly, until children begin to spontaneously ask to create a graph to solve a problem. Some planned and spontaneous graphs we have created answer the following questions:

- ⚹ Should we bake or mash the potatoes we harvested today?
- ⚹ Which garden is your favorite: the sensory garden, the butterfly garden, or the dinosaur garden?
- ⚹ What do you want to buy for the garden with our can-recycling money: a butterfly box, a birdhouse, or a hummingbird feeder?
- ⚹ What do you want to cook for the garden party: basil-cream fettuccini or basil-tomato tarts?
- ⚹ Which do you want to help with next week: filling bird feeders, cleaning and refilling the birdbath, or spraying for bugs?
- ⚹ Did you like or dislike the sage brochette we cooked?

Symbolic graphs should be introduced only after children are confidently and consistently using real and picture graphs. Symbolic graphs use symbols to stand for real things, such as making an *x*, coloring in a square on a piece of graph paper, or applying a sticker to a chart. The potato chart illustrated here used photos of the children to represent their choices of how to cook the potatoes.

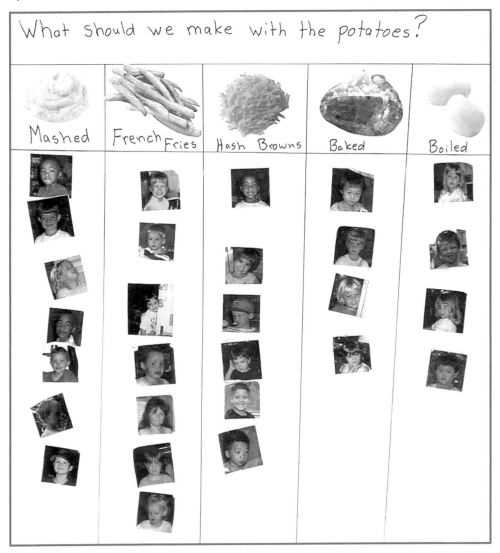

# References

Baratta-Lorton, Mary. 1976. *Mathematics their way.* Menlo Park, Calif.: Addison-Wesley.

Cadwell, Louise Boyd. 1997. *Bringing Reggio Emilia home: An innovative approach to early childhood education.* New York: Teachers College Press.

Curtis, Deb, and Margie Carter. 2000. *The art of awareness.* St. Paul: Redleaf Press.

Davey, Beth. 1983. Think Aloud—Modeling the cognitive processes of reading comprehension. *Journal of Reading,* 27 (1): 44–46.

Helm, Judy Harris, Sally Beneke, and Kathy Steinheimer. 1998. *Windows on learning: Documenting young children's work.* New York: Teachers College Press.

Helm, Judy Harris, and Lilian G. Katz. 2001. *Young investigators: The project approach in the early years.* New York: Teachers College Press.

Jones, Elizabeth, and John Nimmo. 1995. *Emergent curriculum.* Washington, D.C.: NAEYC.

Ogle, Donna. 1986. K-W-L: A teaching model that develops active reading of expository text. *The Reading Teacher,* 39 (6): 564–570.

# 3

# Planning Your Garden

Almost every garden has a theme. There are vegetable gardens, flower gardens, rose gardens, Japanese gardens, and cactus gardens, to name just a few. Our hope is that you will choose a theme for your garden based on the interests of the children in your group. The *K* and *W* steps of the K-W-L process, as well as children's responses to planned fieldwork trips, provide information for making this decision. Some groups will be fascinated with cooking and tasting, which could lend itself to herb and vegetable gardens. Other classes will gravitate toward bright colors and new fragrances, which might lead you to develop some type of flower garden. Another group might be enthralled with the idea of winged visitors and other wildlife, convincing you to use plants that will attract birds, butterflies, or rabbits. You will also want to consider your own curriculum goals and objectives as you think about what theme(s) to focus on for your garden.

In this section we describe five theme gardens in detail and include sample plans from the gardens at Child Development Laboratories (CDL). We also include ideas for other theme gardens and lists of plant suggestions for some of these. The names of plants you find in this section are primarily common names. Since common names vary from region to region, we have listed plants by common name in the text and have referenced the common name to the Latin name in the appendix. If you know the Latin name, you can be certain that you are finding the plant you want.

## Bird and Butterfly Garden

Birds and butterflies are enchanting to children and adults, as well as educational, so attracting them to the garden greatly increases the opportunities for learning. You will probably want a

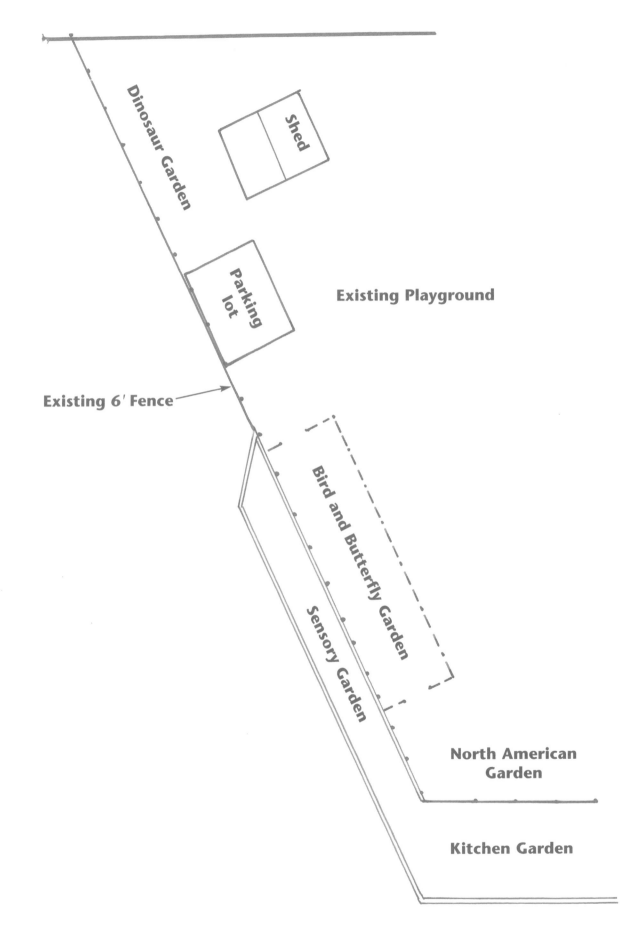

Shed

Dinosaur Garden

Parking lot

Existing Playground

Existing 6' Fence

Bird and Butterfly Garden

Sensory Garden

North American Garden

Kitchen Garden

sunny area for this garden, since most flowers need at least six hours of sunlight to bloom well.

The bird and butterfly garden should contain a variety of annuals, perennials, and herbs, including clusters of colorful, nectar-producing plants in varieties that provide for successive blooms throughout the season. You'll also want to include one or two bushes, which will provide the dense branching needed for birds' nests. Possible choices include lilacs or butterfly bushes, which also lend height to the garden. The butterfly bush has the added advantage of growing quite tall in a single season (up to 8 feet in our area) and blooming throughout the late summer. And they don't call it a butterfly bush for nothing; it really does attract butterflies. The bushes, because they are taller than the children, also provide private spaces where children can spend time alone or with a friend, while remaining within view of adults.

Many flowers will attract butterflies. In our garden, we included bee balm, statice, alyssum, pinks, thyme, basil, sage, and blue salvia. Red salvia has the added attraction of inviting hummingbirds to the garden. You'll probably want to include a birdbath, which will help attract birds, especially in dry weather. Additional features you might want to consider for this garden are butterfly houses, butterfly feeders, hummingbird feeders, birdhouses, and bird feeders.

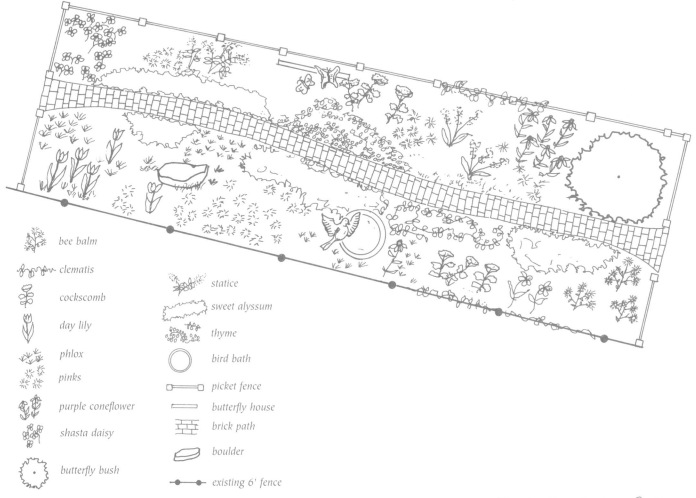

bee balm

clematis

cockscomb

day lily

phlox

pinks

purple coneflower

shasta daisy

butterfly bush

statice

sweet alyssum

thyme

bird bath

picket fence

butterfly house

brick path

boulder

existing 6' fence

## North American Garden

A North American garden focuses on plants that are native to the North American continent and were grown in the Americas by Native peoples before Columbus arrived in 1492. These include corn, pumpkins, popcorn, squash, beans, blanketflower, and many types of gourds. To make the most of the space, include some kind of trellis for the vines to climb. While your playground fence can serve this purpose, you might want to use a separate structure that can double for use in dramatic play.

The highlight of our North American garden is a trellis house, which consists of a wood frame covered with latticeboard. Each summer the base of the trellis house is planted with climbing vines, which cover the house by the end of the summer. Our favorite plants for this use are gourds, because they are so dramatic. They grow quickly and often creep inside the house to grow hanging from the ceiling, much to the delight of the children.

Since most of the plants in this garden are annuals, you can vary the garden design from year to year. Because many of the plants take up a great deal of space and our North American garden is relatively small, we've used the same small patch to plant something new each year. One year the area contained pumpkins, a favorite of the children, as the vines worked hard to take over the playground and would probably have succeeded if it were not for the intervention of little feet. Other years the same area has yielded a patch of closely planted corn, a bean teepee, and a sunflower house.

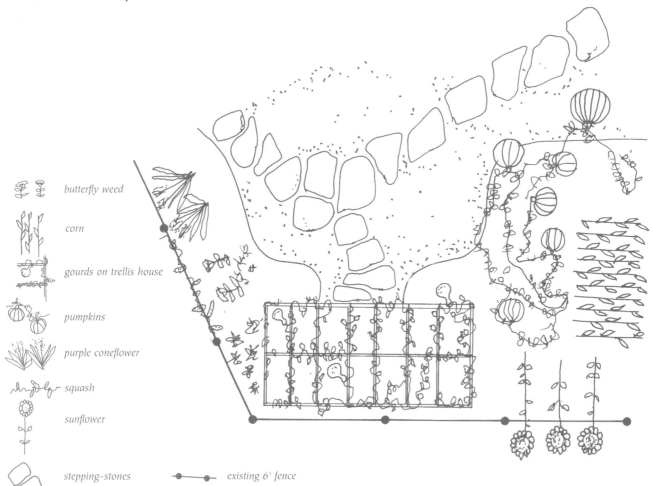

butterfly weed

corn

gourds on trellis house

pumpkins

purple coneflower

squash

sunflower

stepping-stones          existing 6' fence

## Kitchen Garden

Many teachers will want to use their garden to teach how vegetables grow and meet the interests of children who are fascinated by cooking and tasting new foods. The kitchen garden fulfills this purpose. To get maximum use out of this area, you can plant several times throughout the growing season. For instance, spring and fall plantings can include cool-weather plants such as lettuce, spinach, broccoli, cauliflower, and radishes. These plants not only can be planted early or late in the season, but also develop rapidly from seed to edible vegetables, satisfying the shorter attention spans of some children.

Plants that can be grown during the hot summer, and that you will certainly want to include, are tomatoes, green bell and banana peppers, green beans, and cucumbers. Also try eggplant, potatoes, melons, carrots, and onions. We try to include some vegetables that have edible roots, some that have edible leaves, and some that have edible fruit to expose the children to a variety of plant parts as food. We also like to include produce that can be eaten fresh directly out of the garden, as well as vegetables that need to be cooked.

If you have space, you might want to include a small patch of strawberries. These ripen early in the season and the plump, sweet berries will delight most children. However, strawberries do tend to take over the garden, so you will need to periodically pull up the vines to protect the rest of the garden.

Since some of these plants require significant space to grow, you won't be able to plant as closely as you can in some of the other gardens. This can result in more weeds, if you're not careful. Heavily mulch this area to control the weeds, as well as to help the plants retain moisture. Materials that work well for this include wood chips, newspaper, and straw.

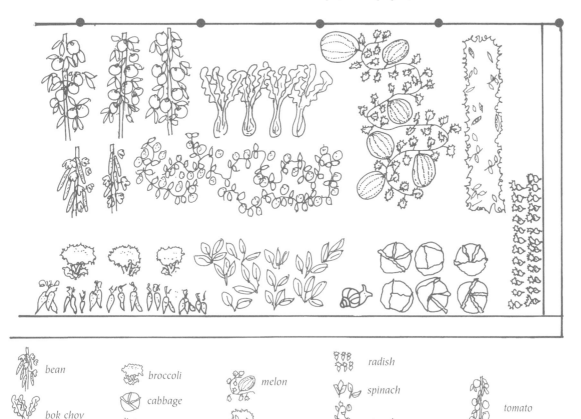

bean

bok choy

broccoli

cabbage

carrot

melon

pea

radish

spinach

strawberry

tomato

## Sensory Garden

A sensory garden offers many learning opportunities for young children. You may choose to divide a sensory garden into five gardens, each dedicated to one of the five senses: sight, sound, taste, touch, and smell. Or you might prefer to intermingle the plants, since many tend to speak to more than one sense, so that you have one large garden. In either case, a sensory garden can be large, but it doesn't need to be. In fact this is one garden that works well in containers: one container dedicated to each of the five senses. Half barrels are perfect for this.

6-20-00

(Alex)

I'm putting one plant in there.

We planted marigolds next to the sunflower house.

Putting flowers in there.

(Jasmine)

### Taste

The taste garden can contain many of the same plants as the kitchen garden, but should focus on those that can be tasted as soon as they are picked. You'll want to include some herbs, since they have strong flavors. Mints are a favorite because they come in many different varieties, which suggest other foods, such as chocolate mint, lemon mint, and lime mint. However, if you plant mint, beware. It grows rampant and will intrude on your other plants if you are not careful. (See sidebar.)

blueberry

cactus

Chinese lantern

dusty miller

geraniums

grasses

lamb's ear

mint

money plant

pansies

sedum

snapdragon

statice

strawflower

zinnia

Berries are also a good choice for this garden. You'll want to find out what plants grow well in your area, but blueberries and blackberries are two possibilities. If you grow blackberries, be sure to get a thornless variety.

Also include some edible flowers. Our favorites are pansies, which grow well here in the cooler weather of spring and fall, and nasturtiums, which we plant during the hot summer. Edible flowers are discussed in more detail in chapter 8.

### Sound

A sound garden is a bit of a challenge, since people don't really think of plants as making noise. This garden works best when teachers encourage children to listen for sounds that exist beyond the plants: the buzzing of bees and chirping of birds, for example. However, you will also want to include plants that make a rattling sound if shaken when dried, such as Chinese lanterns and money plant. Flowers that have dryer petals, such as statice and strawflower, also make noise when rubbed. In addition, you can include grasses that rustle in the breeze. Devices such as wind chimes add to the auditory appeal of this garden.

### Touch

Plants that are fuzzy, prickly, or spongy make up a touch garden. Favorites for touching are lamb's ear, dusty miller, cockscomb, and different varieties of sedum. Also include plants that change when handled. For instance, children quickly learned how to manipulate snapdragons by gently squeezing in the right place to make them open and "snap" shut.

You might want to include a plant or two that has prickles or thorns as well. A small, hardy rose shrub or a cactus plant would serve this purpose. If you include one of these or another thorny plant, place it in the back of the garden where it is not likely to be accidentally bumped, and educate the children about safe handling practices.

### Sight

Bright, bold, cheery flowers dominate the sight garden. If you plan well, you can orchestrate a succession of flowers throughout the growing season. In the early spring, tulips are a joy to winter-weary eyes, as are other flowers that grow from bulbs, such as daffodils and crocuses. As summer progresses, flowers such as zinnias, strawflowers, marigolds, hollyhocks, and geraniums can take their place. By including mums in this garden, you will also have blooms as summer turns to fall.

## Dealing with Invasive Plants

Some plants, such as mints, tend to grow rampant and invade parts of the garden where you do not want them to be. Once they get started, it's hard to stop them. To avoid this problem, you can plant them in containers. You can also limit the space they have to grow by following these steps:

1. Cut out the bottom from a five-gallon bucket or other deep container.
2. Dig a hole in your garden deep enough to hold the container.
3. Place the container in the ground with about one inch protruding above the ground.
4. Fill the container with soil and plant your invasive plant inside. This will keep the roots from spreading outside the container.

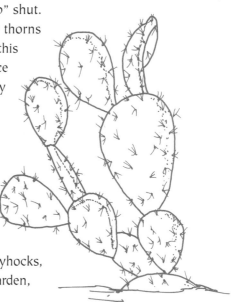

Also consider plants with interesting leaves. Large-leafed plants, such as cannas or hostas attract attention. Some sedums actually look like rocks. Consider colored foliage as well, such as coleus.

Our sight garden is one of our favorites, and certainly the one that brings us the most notice. These plants attract attention from passersby and the showiness of our sight garden is a sensation from the distant road. It never fails to delight us as we drive past.

### Smell

Highly fragrant plants, such as herbs, are perfect for the smell garden. You may also want to add fragrant flowers, such as scented geraniums or hardy shrub roses. Be careful to select a variety of plants with distinct fragrances.

The scent garden provides for many pleasurable experiences beyond simply smelling plants and flowers. Herbs, such as sage and basil, call for attention and provide new experiences throughout the season. They require frequent deadheading (cutting back the flowers to encourage continued growth), which gives children opportunities to cut flowers. In addition, we have found other uses for the flowers, from tasting them outright to dipping sage blossoms in batter and deep-frying them. We also used these herbs to make food, such as herb butter and basil-tomato tart.

## Dinosaur Garden

Dinosaurs fascinate many young children, so a garden designed with dinosaurs in mind is a natural attraction. Our dinosaur garden was inspired by some sculptures we had from previous classroom experiences. One of our parents, who taught art, had his class assemble two large dinosaur frames from rebar. These were initially overlaid with chicken wire and covered, by the children, with papier-mâché. However, by the time we built the garden, the papier-mâché and chicken wire had been removed and only the frames remained. These seemed to be perfect for garden trellises, so we decided to use them to suggest a dinosaur theme in an area that was in deep shade.

Both sunny and shaded areas work well for the dinosaur garden. We chose plants with large leaves to give the garden a larger-than-life feel that would give children the experience of lush, jungle-like vegetation. Especially appropriate to this garden are plants that tower over the children. If you live in a warm, humid climate, it should be easy to find plants that meet these requirements.

You might want to combine plants from ancient families, such as *ginkgo biloba* or southern magnolia (large trees) or many ferns, with more modern plants that have a "Jurassic" look.

Love-lies-bleeding and elephant amaranth, for instance, might be appropriate. For our purposes and with our climate limitations, hosta and astilbe worked well. We also included New Guinea impatiens, which added color to this garden.

To extend the dinosaur theme in our garden, we made dinosaur stepping-stones for the pathway. Karen, using a photograph of an actual iguanodon footprint from one of our reference books, made patterns for right and left feet for the stepping-stones. The father of one of our children used this drawing to make the molds, which were filled with concrete to make the stones. If you don't know anyone who has the resources to do this, you can dig a hole the shape of a dinosaur foot in a box of wet sand, and use this as a mold for the concrete.

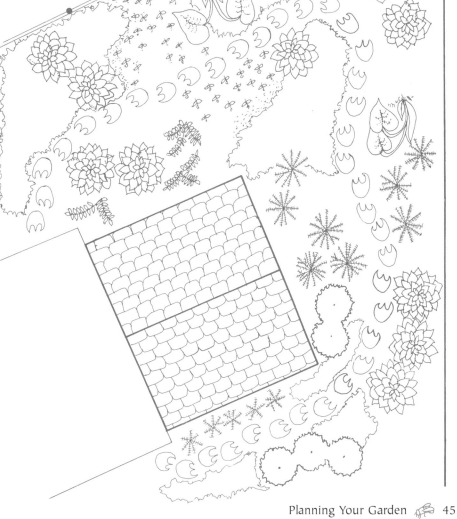

astilbe

big leaf hosta

canna

fern

New Guinea impatiens

variegated hosta

violets

dinosaur footprint
stepping-stone

dinosaur sculpture

## More Ideas for Themes

Let your interests and those of your children be your guide as you explore different types of gardens. Also, look to your community for ideas. You may want to select a cultural theme, especially if you have a significant number of children who come from a particular culture. For example, you might plant a Chinese vegetable garden, a garden with foods specific to Mexican cooking, or a garden with plants introduced to this country by African Americans. Japanese gardens are beautiful additions and can take advantage of small spaces. These tranquil spots can encourage children to slow down, observe, and think. Parents are good resources if you decide to focus on a specific culture. They will be able to help you decide what to grow and may be able to lead you to sources for seeds that are less common in this country. See the sidebar for suggested plants for some culture-based gardens.

Another common theme is the rainbow garden, with flowers arranged by color. If you have space, you can make the garden in the traditional rainbow shape. However, if room doesn't allow for this, you might consider arranging colorful stepping-stones in a rainbow pattern inside a square or rectangular garden and adding a pot of gold (spray-painted gold gravel) as the landing at the end of the garden. Themes similar to the rainbow are the crayon garden, with plants selected to represent crayon colors and the color wheel, which can provide a living art lesson. If you have a great deal of space, you might want to try an alphabet garden, which includes flowers whose names start with each letter of the alphabet. The sidebar on the next page includes a list of plants for this garden.

One of our favorite themes is the pizza garden, which contains many ingredients common to pizza and other Italian dishes. We've planted tomatoes, green peppers, oregano, basil, onions, and parsley in our pizza garden. We also included signet marigolds, an edible flower that is an interesting addition to pizza. Some people plant the pizza garden in a large round area, with paths bisecting the circle to suggest pizza slices (see the drawing), but it can be planted in any shape, and actually makes a great container garden. The herbs can be planted in small pots and the tomatoes, green peppers, and onions in large pots or half barrels.

Specific colors, such as blues and whites, can also constitute a theme. If you limit the color scheme, you'll want to select plants with various shades of the chosen color, various textures of leaves and flowers, and different growth habits. This will give you diversity in height, width, times of bloom, and other characteristics that will make your garden interesting.

Children's stories can suggest a garden theme as well. For instance, a Peter Rabbit garden would include the plants Peter comes in contact with during his adventures, such as lettuce, beans, radishes, parsley, cabbages, blackberries, and chamomile. Let the children examine the pictures in the book to come up with ideas for decorating the garden.

---

### Suggestions for Plants to Include in Culture-based Themes

#### African American Garden
*These plants were introduced to America by African Americans.*

cucumber
okra
peanuts
black-eyed peas
watermelon
geraniums
collards
sesame
sorghum

#### Hispanic American Garden

Mexican sage
Mexican tea
tomatoes
tomatillo
peppers
cilantro
eggplant

#### Asian American Garden

Chinese okra
asparagus bean (yard-long bean)
pac choi
snow peas
Chinese cabbage

*Source: 4-H Children's Garden at Michigan State University*

---

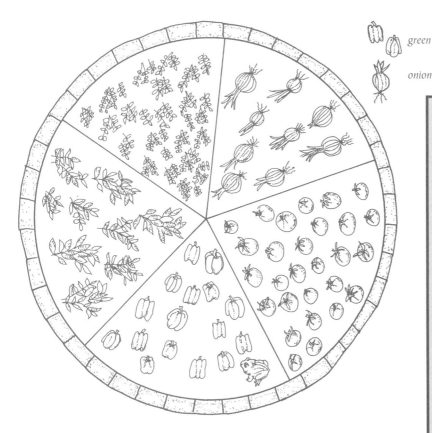

green pepper    oregano    tomatoes

onion    parsley    stone edging

## Alphabet Garden

A  alyssum, astilbe
B  bee balm, butterfly bush, basil, beans, broccoli
C  chamomile, chrysanthemum, corn, cauliflower, carrots, Chinese lanterns
D  dusty miller, daisy, 'Dragon's Blood' sedum, dill
E  eggplant, echinacea (coneflower), evening primrose
F  ferns, four-o'clock, flax
G  geranium, gourd, garlic
H  hollyhock, hosta
I  impatiens, Indian blanket flower
J  Jacob's ladder, Johnny-jump-up, Job's tears
K  kale, kiss-me-over-the-garden-Kate
L  love-in-a-puff, lettuce, lemon balm, lamb's ear, love-lies-bleeding
M  marigold, melons, mints, money plant
N  nasturtium, nigella (love-in-a-mist)
O  onions, oregano
P  pansy, pinks, pumpkin, popcorn, potatoes, peppers, parsley, petunia
Q  Queen Anne's lace, quaking grass, quicksilver
R  radishes, red hot pokers, rose, rosemary
S  salvia, sage, sunflower, strawflowers, statice, snapdragons, sedum
T  thyme, tomatoes
U  unicorn plant
V  verbena, violet
W  wild ginger, wormwood
X  xanthisma (Star of Texas)
Y  yarrow, yams, yucca
Z  zinnia

Another suggestion is a dye garden. This would include plants that can be used to make dyes, such as marigolds, coreopsis, zinnia, cosmos, dahlias, tansy, indigo, and blackberries. Children may choose to dye cloth, but can also make paints out of the plants in this garden. You'll want to locate this garden near a shady spot with space for activities. You could include large boulders for sitting (or for pounding berries) or old crates to use as tables.

Whatever theme you choose, you shouldn't feel you are stuck with it forever. Many plants will need to be replanted yearly, and perennials can always be removed if they are no longer wanted. New groups of children will have different interests, so you should consider your garden a constantly evolving learning center. As you gain experience, you will find there are some plants you would never be without and some that are so much trouble you don't want to mess with them. This is part of the joy of gardening.

## Involving Children in the Planning Process

As you begin the process of planning and building your garden, you will find that much of the work needs to be done by adults. It's easy to leave the children out of this stage, but we encourage you to include them as much as you can. While you plan your garden, you can continue to explore gardens with the children through books, fieldwork trips, and indoor activities. We've included suggestions throughout this chapter to help you keep the children involved as the adults plan and perform the heavy labor of constructing the garden—they're in the boxes with the grasshopper on top. Topics in the rest of this chapter include

- ⊛ ways to approach planning the garden
- ⊛ factors to consider in selecting the garden site
- ⊛ advantages and disadvantages of different types of gardens

## Deciding on Your Approach

There are two approaches to developing a garden, each with its own challenges and rewards. The first is to decide what you want to grow and then try to find the space to grow it. While this method may leave you with overcrowded tomatoes or a haphazard arrangement of flowers,

you and the children will learn from your experiences. Since learning is the purpose of any school garden, there is no failure in making mistakes as you tackle the garden head-on.

The second approach is to plan the garden carefully before deciding what plants to grow. If you want a garden that will become a permanent part of your program, you might want to put more thought into your planning, including other adults and parents in helping you come up with a design that will make the most of the space you have and enhance the appearance of your facility. You might also want to consult books or magazines on this topic to assist you with the process. For an example of the difference a well-planned garden can make to your outdoor space, see the photos below, showing a corner of our playground before the garden was built, in the spring when the trellis house is visible, and in the summer when the vines covering the house are in full riotous growth.

Our main regret, as we look back at the history of our garden, is that we were too ambitious. Our garden is very large and takes a great deal of maintenance. We strongly recommend that, if you have a large area you wish to turn into a garden, you start with about 100 square feet and develop it a little at a time. If you increase the size a little bit each year, you will know when you have reached the limit of what you can easily maintain.

## Selecting the Garden Site

Where you decide to put your garden will depend on what space you have available. Some schools have lots of unused land, while others have almost no space at all. Don't despair if you have no obvious gardening area. A container garden can fit on a small patio or even on a rooftop. If there is absolutely no outdoor space available, you can still garden inside. There are several aspects of your space you'll need to evaluate before making a decision about where to put the garden. These include accessibility, sun exposure, water access, soil quality, drainage, and existing structures and utilities. As you examine the available space, you will also want to think about what type of garden will work best for you.

## Accessibility

Probably the factor that will most impact the benefits of gardening with your class is accessibility. If you can't easily get to the garden, chances are it won't become an integral part of your classroom. We strongly recommend putting the garden on your playground, if space allows. In fact, a container garden on the playground may be better than the most elaborate garden a block away. The greatest benefit of the playground garden is that it allows teachers and other adults to work with some children in the garden while others are occupied with other types of play. It also provides children the opportunity to interact with the garden alone or with a friend. Since the best gardening experiences happen with individual children or in small groups, the playground garden provides the best opportunities for intense learning.

If you can't put your garden directly on the playground, other spaces on the school lot should be considered. Again, these will be more accessible than gardens further away. You may be able to incorporate a landscaping feature to your advantage. For example, one of our local elementary schools used the inside of a circle drive for a garden area, enhancing their landscaping in the process. Finally, if there is no space on the grounds of the school, look at other nearby areas. Do remember, though, that if you select a spot away from the school, you'll need a greater commitment to providing the children with opportunities to visit the garden.

## Kid Tip

As you study gardens with the children, help them identify the different features. Do the gardens have paths? Are there garden structures, such as trellises, for the plants to climb on? Does the garden include decorations, such as statues or sculptures? Are there birdbaths or other structures to attract animals? How are the plants arranged? Have them record their findings through drawings or dictation. Post their work in the classroom. You can refer back to these discoveries as the children discuss what features they want in their garden.

Read *Princess Chamomile's Garden* (Oram and Varley 2000). Although a bit fanciful, this book describes how Princess Chamomile (a rabbit) designs a garden and how the garden is built over a period of time. Teachers can use the book to lead children into a discussion of what features they would like to have in their garden.

In addition, bring in garden catalogs and encourage the children to look at the pictures and study flowers and vegetables. Children can begin making suggestions about what they would like to plant. You might want to make a simple graph with photographs from the catalogs so children can vote on their favorite plants.

Involve children in tasting vegetables and herbs to give them some ideas of what they can grow in their garden.

If you have selected a garden theme, guide the children in exploring plants that will fit your theme. You can graph this as well with a two-column chart. For instance, if you've decided to plant a kitchen garden, one column can be titled "plants we can eat" and the other "plants we can't eat." Children can cut photos from catalogs to paste in each column.

If adults are involved in the garden design, post plans in the classroom for children and parents to review. Encourage the children to draw similar designs of how they think the garden should look. Post these in the classroom as well.

## Sun Exposure

Most vegetables and flowering plants require at least six hours of direct sunlight every day. You will be able to grow a wider variety of plants if you can provide a sunny place for them. Watch sun patterns throughout the day. There may be areas that are not in full sun all day, but that receive sun during the morning or afternoon.

If you don't have any space that provides direct sun, you will still be able to garden, but your options will be more limited. Some plants tolerate, or actually prefer, shade, and these plants can provide you with a cool, lush area for quiet contemplation, art activities, or journal writing. A shade garden makes such a nice refuge during the hot days of summer that you might want to consider planting one, even if you have a great sunny spot.

## Water Access

Your garden must have access to water. Unless you live in an area where consistent rainfall is guaranteed, you'll want to have a water hydrant nearby with sufficient garden hoses, sprinklers, or drip hoses to provide water directly after planting and throughout the season. You'll also want to set a schedule to be sure that plants are watered on a regular basis. A deep watering once or twice a week is better than frequent, light applications, because it forces the roots to grow deeper in search of water. For this reason, if you let children water, with either the hose or with watering cans, you'll probably need to follow up with the sprinkler or drip hose to make sure the plants receive enough water. While watering once a week is usually sufficient in our area once plants are established, you'll want to talk with experienced gardeners in your area to find out what will be best for you.

## Soil

Unfortunately, the soil on many school playgrounds is not the best quality. Years of little feet pushing down on the earth compacts the soil so little will grow there. Fortunately, the more you work with your soil, the richer it will become. An ideal soil includes sand, clay, silt, and organic matter in amounts to make it loose, friable (easily crumbled), and easy to work. Such good, loamy soil will provide essential nutrients, air, and water to your plants.

Soil is usually general to the region in which you live. Here, in southern Illinois, our soil runs to heavy clay. Other areas may be sandy. If you ask around, you can easily find out what kind of soil is common to your area.

### Kid Tip

Children can become investigators as you examine your area for sun exposure. One idea is to make a simple chart with two columns. Write "sun" at the top of one column and "no sun" at the top of the other. Now place an object in the area you are considering. Once every hour, throughout the day, check the area with the children to see if the object is in the sun. (You might want to use a timer to remind you when it's time to check.) If the object is in the sun, the children can place a check mark in the "sun" column. If it is not, then they check the "no sun" column. At the end of the day, add up the marks. If you have six marks in the "sun" column (six hours of sun), the area should be a good place for plants that require full sun. If you have just a few marks, the area might work better for plants that require partial shade. If you only have one or two marks, you would probably want to look for plants that do best in shade for this area.

Often you will find that the soil has changed due to development, erosion, or compaction. In any case, you'll want to evaluate the soil in the garden area to see if it is suitable for planting. The best way to do this is to pick up a handful. (If you can't do so, the soil needs work.) Squeeze the soil. If it becomes a tight, sticky mass, you probably have a lot of clay in your soil. If it won't hold a shape at all, you most likely have a lot of sand. The ideal soil will mold to your hand when squeezed, then fall apart when you let go. If your soil meets this description, you are one lucky gardener. Most of us have to work on our soil.

Soil with too much clay in it is hard to work. The small pores in the soil don't let in enough oxygen for the plants. Heavy clay can also cause drainage problems, as it tends to hold water. Sandy soil causes the opposite problem. Water and nutrients run through it so quickly that the plants don't have time to absorb them. Soil with the right proportions of both takes advantage of the good qualities of each component. The clay helps hold the water and provides strength to firmly root the plants, while the sand provides adequate drainage. Good garden soil is easy to work, even for the small hands of preschool children.

If you find that your soil needs work, you can easily amend it by adding topsoil, sand, or organic materials, such as peat moss and compost. For instance, if you have heavy clay soil, you can add sand to it to make it more workable and improve drainage. If your soil is sandy, you can add clay to improve the texture. Humus improves any soil. It makes clay soil more friable, improves the water retention of sandy soil and, in the process, makes all soil more fertile. Humus-producing organic materials include compost, peat moss, ground-up leaves, rotted sawdust, and straw. If you feel you need assistance in determining how to improve your soil, consult a master gardener or your local nursery for assistance. And if the idea of digging up and reworking your soil seems totally overwhelming, you can avoid the whole ordeal by building raised beds or having a container garden. We'll discuss this in more detail later in this chapter.

## Soil pH

When evaluating an area for a garden, you may also need to consider soil pH. The pH relates to the alkaline/acid ratio of the soil. Most plants prefer a pH in the neutral range of 6.0 to 7.5, although some plants, such as

blueberries, azaleas, and potatoes, prefer a slightly acidic soil. You don't necessarily need to analyze your soil for pH before you start to garden, but if your garden doesn't seem to be growing well it makes sense to check. Simple testing kits are available at most garden centers. For more advanced testing, you can contact your local extension service. If you have soil with poor pH, you can make it more alkaline by adding lime. Or you can add an acidic-forming fertilizer or pine needles to reduce the pH and make it more acidic. If you need to adjust your pH, we suggest that you consult with a local nursery to determine how much of a supplement you need to add to your specific site.

### Kid Tip

Children can study the natural rainfall a site receives by using a rain gauge and recording any accumulation of water after a rain. You can also test your sprinkler with a rain gauge. Place the gauge in the area covered by the sprinkler, turn on the water, and check every fifteen minutes. See how long it takes the rain gauge to collect an inch of water. This is the length of time you will need to leave it on to thoroughly water your garden.

## Drainage

Even with the best garden soil, you can have problems with drainage. The lay of the land or man-made structures can cause water to drain into an area and settle there for long periods of time. This can mean death for plants, which need moisture but cannot obtain oxygen when the roots are covered in water. Carefully check your garden area to be sure that the drainage is sufficient. Consider runoff from rooftops and placement of gutter downspouts. Watch the area over a period of time to see whether water collects there.

If you have an area that would be ideal, except for drainage problems, you don't necessarily need to avoid it. Instead, consider building raised beds, which will provide sufficient drainage, or developing a wet area with plants that tolerate wet feet. You can also put in a drainage system, but this may entail more work than you want to do.

## Utilities

Be sure to find out whether there are any underground utilities in the desired garden site before you start to dig. You don't want to cut an underground cable or have your garden destroyed because workers have to dig it up to access underground utilities. Call the utility companies before you finalize your plans. They will come out and mark any utilities in the area. Remember, utility lines can be placed at surprisingly shallow levels. Also, be careful not to plant too close to an air-conditioning unit. The hot air from such an appliance will create an unhealthy environment for your plants and the loud noise will be distracting.

## Types of Gardens

As you study your site, you'll want to be thinking about what type of garden you want to build. There are four basic choices: a ground-level garden, a raised bed, a mounded garden, or a container garden. You may want to use only one type of garden or you may choose to include several types. We have both raised-bed and in-ground gardens on our preschool playground, while we use containers in our toddler area.

## The Ground-Level Garden

A ground-level or in-ground garden is what most people think of when they picture a garden. In fact, what people often envision is the traditional in-ground garden with vegetables in neatly spaced rows. A ground-level garden takes advantage of the space and soil available. It works well if you have good soil and good drainage. Most of the work goes into digging and enriching the soil, and this may be more economical since most of the cost is in soil amendments rather than building materials.

While ground-level gardens have many advantages, the straight-row garden is probably not your best choice. When you plant in rows, you maximize the opportunities for weeds that eagerly pop up in the spaces between your plants. In addition, it's not a very efficient use of your space. We prefer an approach that spaces plants closer together, while providing pathways for children to access the garden. An excellent resource for getting the most out of your gardening space is *Square Foot Gardening* (Bartholomew 1981).

### Kid Tip

Here's an experiment you can do with children to see if you have good drainage. Dig a hole 1 foot wide and 1 foot deep. Fill it with water. Watch the hole and see how long it takes for the water to drain. (Also, watch the children to be sure they don't fall into the hole.) If the water is still there in an hour, you have poor drainage.

As you plan your in-ground garden, think about where you can put paths and what materials you will use for them. Materials such as bricks, stones, or concrete stepping-stones are durable but can be costly if you are unable to obtain donations. Less expensive choices include wood mulch, straw, sawdust, gravel, or even wooden boards. While these materials will have to be replaced from time to time, they work well at defining the pathway and keeping down weeds.

Since you're working with children, the planting areas will need to be narrower than if you were planting for adults. We recommend that the planting space between paths be limited to about 18 inches if the space is accessible from only one side or 3 feet if it is accessible from both sides. This will ensure that children can reach the plants. If you are planting some perennials that will require minimum maintenance and that will be placed at the back of the bed, you might increase this to 2 feet. Just remember that children will not be able to reach these plants without venturing off the path.

The major advantage of the ground-level garden is that it's simple. It doesn't require you to build a frame or to cart in large masses of soil. You have most of what you need right there. The greatest disadvantage of such a garden is that, depending on your soil condition, it may be somewhat labor intensive the first year. However, properly preparing the bed is the key to producing a successful garden with healthy plants. It is well worth the time and effort you take to create good growing conditions for your plants.

## The Raised-Bed Garden

A raised bed is a gardening area developed using construction materials, such as landscape timbers or treated wood, to raise the height of the planting area. There are many advantages to raised beds. They're easier to reach, since you don't have to bend all the way down to the ground to plant and weed. They are also ideal if you want a garden that is accessible to people who use wheelchairs or have other mobility impairments. (For more information on making your garden more accessible to people with disabilities, read

*The Enabling Garden* by Gene Rothert.) Raised beds are easier to maintain, since they tend to keep weeds in check better than the in-ground garden. It's easier to control the composition of the soil, since you are adding the ingredients to create your planting medium. And it's easier to keep the children from accidentally trampling the plants, since they are above foot level. In addition, the beds usually drain well, since they are above the ground level. The disadvantage of the raised bed is that you'll have to supply the materials to build the wall of the garden as well as the soil to fill the bed. This may also be somewhat labor intensive, depending on what you use to build the sides of your beds.

## The Mounded-Bed Garden

Mounded beds, or berms, are much like raised beds, only without the walls. They can be a good choice if you don't have access to materials for building walls or if you just want a more natural appearance. A berm may be especially pleasing if you have a flat, uninteresting space for your garden. Berms can be arranged in any shape, and the curves that are common to mounded beds make the garden visually enticing, while the height brings the flowers up to a level where they are more noticeable. Improved drainage is also an advantage of berms, although you will have to be careful, since they also shed water from the sides easily. A deep layer of mulch can help control this problem.

## Container Gardens

A container, for gardening purposes, is any portable item (which may be heavy, especially when filled with a soil mix) that is used to plant in. The main advantage of container gardening is that you can garden in areas that lack a soil base or in small areas, such as a patio.

5·10·00

Hunter, Maggie and Miriam planted potatoes. We planted blue potatoes. We put them inside a tire. As they grow, we'll add more tires so they'll grow more roots and more potatoes

Another advantage is that containers are easy to maintain. You have complete control over the soil mixture, and weeds are few and far between. The height of containers makes them easy to work in and increases the visual effect, as they bring the plants closer to eye level. In addition, small to medium-size containers can be moved to follow the sun or rearranged throughout the season as different plants come into their prime. If you have a long break, smaller containers can also travel home with children for care while the school is closed.

## The Final Choice

As you study your site, you may find that you have an obvious garden space available to you, an area that seems perfect for a garden. Or you may need to spend some time evaluating what is available and choosing the best of several poor alternatives. Under extreme circumstances, where you have absolutely no outdoor space available or where the outdoors is not safe for children, you may choose to plant an indoor garden. Your choice will depend on the location and the resources available to you.

No matter what space you select, it is possible to plant a garden that will serve your needs, whether it's a traditional flower and vegetable garden in full sun or a secluded shade garden, and whether it's dug into the ground, built in raised beds, or confined to containers.

## References

Bartholomew, Mel. 1981. *Square foot gardening*. Emmaus, Pa.: Rodale Press.

Oram, Hiawyn, and Susan Varley. 2000. *Princess Chamomile's garden*. New York: Dutton Books.

Rothert, Gene. 1994. *The enabling garden: Creating barrier-free gardens*. Dallas, Tex.: Taylor Publishing Company.

# 4

# Building Your Garden

Once you've decided where to build your garden and what kind of garden you want, you'll be ready to start the process of building the garden. Now it's time to get organized. Remember that spending time planning and preparing for your garden pays off in making the actual work go more smoothly.

Make a plan for preparing the area, obtaining materials, and securing labor. If you are on a low budget, this is the time to solicit volunteers and donations. Use your garden design as a tool to build interest among staff, parents, local nurseries, and garden centers when asking for their assistance. Our design was useful in creating enthusiasm, and when others saw that we had a specific plan, they were eager to help bring it to fruition. Several local nurseries donated plants for our garden and a number of mail-order companies sent us seeds. In addition, the university and a landscape design class donated labor for bed preparation and construction. Many parents donated plants or materials and helped with the planting. You will be surprised at how many people are willing to help, if asked.

## The Children's Role in Building the Garden

Now, as you begin the actual construction of the garden, the children will want to be involved. And you will want to involve them as much as possible to ensure that they feel ownership of the garden. Some of the construction work will need to be completed by adults, but children can participate in their own way as you begin your work.

When you begin laying out the plan on the ground, the children can assist in staking and flagging the area. They can observe as adults build the beds and can keep track of the progress in their garden journal. Be sure to take some photographs of the site before you begin, as well as at various stages of development. These will be valuable as the children recall the sequence of the garden installation. If the children keep a running record of how their garden was built, the photographs, drawings, and dictation can be used for posterboards that will inform others about your garden.

Children can also assist in moving soil and additives to the garden. They can fill small wheelbarrows with these materials and move them to the garden area. If you take time to prepare the bed, children can also assist in mixing the materials in the beds. If you are going to be gardening in containers, the children can mix soil ingredients in a large container or wheelbarrow and then help fill the containers with potting mix. Children can also spend time exploring the soil and examining living creatures that are stirred up in the process of building the garden.

## Constructing Different Types of Gardens

Once you know what kind of garden you want to build and you have secured the needed materials, you're ready to start. Following, you will find basic instructions for preparing each type of garden: ground level, raised bed, mounded bed, and container. We have also included some suggestions for indoor gardens.

### Ground-Level Gardens

There are two approaches to choose from as you consider preparing your planting area. If the area is full of invasive weeds or aggressive grass (such as nutsedge or Bermuda grass), you may want to spray a chemical herbicide to kill the growth. If you decide this is necessary, identify the plants and seek professional advice on the type of herbicide, the amount to use, the timing of the application, and precautions to take. Be sure to let your advisor know that you are dealing with a children's garden. Following proper precautions is critical for the safety of the children, the environment, and any adults involved in the project. Plan ahead. Most chemicals take ten days to two weeks to take effect and a second application may be necessary. Do not apply the herbicide when children are present. You will probably want to spray at the beginning of a weekend or a long break to give the herbicide time to break down.

The second approach is to skip the spray application and either remove the sod manually or begin turning soil over as is, leaving the existing vegetation to be used as a green fertilizer. This is preferable if you aren't worried about existing plants invading the garden. To remove the sod, use a flat-tipped spade to separate it from the soil an inch or two below the surface of the grass.

After you have decided which approach to use, and after the herbicide has taken effect, if you elected to use one, it's time to turn over the soil. (This is a good time to invite parents for a workday.) Outline the area with string or spray paint. Using a shovel or spading fork, dig down 12 to 16 inches. Turn the soil over, leaving it in large clods if you have clay soil. The purpose of this procedure is to loosen the soil, allowing plant roots to penetrate and to improve water drainage. Continue working this way until the entire outlined area is turned over. This will go much faster if several people work together.

The next step is to add organic matter to the overturned soil to a depth of 6 to 8 inches. We were fortunate that our university stockpiles grass and leaf clippings throughout the year to use as compost. We had several loads of this delivered and we spread it all over our planting areas. Check around to see if someone in your community can provide you with compost. If not, you can purchase peat moss to add to the soil. Also add any other supplements your previous research has determined you need.

Once the organic matter is roughly spread over the area, use a rototiller to break up the large clods and to work the organic matter into the soil. (It's likely you will be able to find someone who has a rototiller that you can borrow, but if not you will probably be able to rent one at a local rental store.) Go over the bed twice, the second time at a right angle to the first. Don't be concerned if the rototiller blades do not reach to the depth of the turned-over soil. By following this procedure, you will create an environment where healthy plants can grow and children can plant using hand trowels. When you're finished tilling, your bed is ready for planting.

## Raised Beds

Proper preparation of the raised bed is similar to that of the in-ground garden. First, you'll want to select the material for the "wall" of the bed. The material may be selected for aesthetic reasons or because it fits your budget. For instance, native stones are attractive and you may be able to get them free or at a low cost. Other materials you could use include concrete blocks, landscape timbers, or pressure-treated wood. Many gardening companies even sell kits to make raised beds. Scrap lumber can be used if more durable materials are not available, but will not last as long as treated wood. If you use scrap lumber, watch out for splinters and old nails. Do not use new railroad ties for your raised beds. The creosote with which they are treated is toxic to plants and may irritate skin. If you use old timbers, be sure they won't easily splinter. We recommend using pressure-treated wood, since it contains compounds that will seal out moisture and inhibit rotting. You can use untreated wood, but it will need to be replaced within a short period of time. You'll want to consider the safety and longevity of any material you use.

No matter what material you select, you'll want to think seriously about the height and width of the bed before construction. Avoid building a bed that is too high for children to reach

into or for you to observe over. The maximum height should be 24 inches. We used a raised-bed for the garden area outside our playground fence to improve the soil and slightly change the height. Our raised bed is only 6 inches high and is made of 8-by-8-inch landscape timbers in 8-foot lengths. After rototilling the area to break up the hard crust of soil underneath, we buried the timbers 2 inches in the ground for stability.

The width of the bed is also important. For young children, the best width for a freestanding bed is no more than 3 feet (and that's pushing it for very young children), since children have such a short reach and will need to reach the middle of the bed. If the bed is accessible from only one side, don't exceed 18 inches. These widths may vary with age groups, and exception may be made if the plantings are to be shrubs or perennials with a wide spread. If the bed is much wider, the children will need to be able to actually get in the garden and it might be better to have a shallower frame. The width of our raised bed is 8 feet, obviously too deep for a child to reach into. However, groupings of plants were carefully placed to allow children to walk on the wood-chip mulch to reach the vegetation. The children sit on the edge of the bed while working along the outside. Still, if given the chance to do it over again, we might choose narrow beds that could be reached from the outside and on both sides.

You will want to till the soil to improve the texture before you start building your bed. However, you won't need to turn the soil over, since you're raising the height. After you till and build the walls to the bed, you'll want to fill your bed with a combination of topsoil and organic matter. We filled our raised bed with the composted grass and leaf clippings provided by the university, and because this was well-aged we didn't add topsoil or other amendments. However, it is typically recommended that you do so. One suggestion is to add 2 parts topsoil to 1 part peat moss and 1 part compost. You might want to check with local gardeners or your garden center before deciding what mixture to use. One of the advantages of the raised bed is being able to control your planting medium, so this is your chance to mix up a soil that will be most favorable for your plants.

Fill the bed so that the planting medium comes to within 2 inches of the top of the bed, after it is raked and lightly compacted. This will ensure that the soil won't spill out, and you will still have room to add mulch to the bed. Once the bed is filled, you're ready to plant.

## Mounded Beds

To build a mounded bed, first decide what shape you want it to be. With the children, you can play around with a garden hose or a long rope to make an outline for your garden. This is also a good way to determine how wide the bed should be, as you can have the children practice reaching into the space inside the hose. (If you do this without the children, the maximum widths should be the same as for the raised bed.) Experiment with different shapes. One benefit of the berm is that it can take almost any form. Once you have finalized your plans, outline the area by cutting into the soil around the outside with a spade.

Till the area, either with a rototiller or by hand with a spading fork. Then slowly add the materials with which you will fill the bed. (Use the same topsoil and organic material you would use for the raised bed.) Do this in layers, mixing the ingredients together after each layer with a tiller or a shovel. Your finished bed should be between 1 and 2 feet at its highest point.

Because mounded beds allow water to run off, you'll want to mulch the beds heavily (this also keeps the soil from eroding). We also suggest drip hoses for mounded beds, since they distribute water a little at a time and minimize runoff. These should be installed *under* the mulch.

## Container Gardens

The possibilities are endless when it comes to container gardening. Obvious choices are flower pots, troughs, and window boxes, which are available for purchase in a large range of sizes and several different materials. (If you use pots, buy plastic rather than terra-cotta. The moisture in terra-cotta pots evaporates too quickly to make them a good choice for school gardens.) However, any container can be used for gardening as long as it is strong enough to hold the plants and soil, is safe for children to garden in, and has sufficient drainage holes. Pots, pails, watering cans, and even coffee cans make good small containers. If you want something larger, try old car or tractor tires, wooden crates, or half-barrels. An old, but solid, plastic swimming pool that leaks is a good choice. If you're lucky, you may even come across a damaged canoe or other small boat that can easily be transformed into a garden. Your only limit is your imagination.

If you're going to place your containers on a patio or permanent surface, select containers that have bottoms. If you convert objects from other uses to gardening, be sure to drill drainage holes. A drill with a ½-inch bit will work for drilling several holes in smaller containers, but if you have large containers use a 1-inch hole-saw, which can be attached to a drill. You want the water to drain easily so that your plants don't sit in wet soil. Otherwise you risk root rot and unhealthy plant growth.

We put another tire on the potato tower. Now there are four tires. The potatoes are still growing taller.

We planted the potato plants. We covered some more dirt on it. Because it had to grow.

To make your garden most interesting, select a variety of containers in different sizes. This will also help when it comes to finding the right-sized receptacle for each plant.

Be careful in matching the size of the pot to the plant and remember to consider the mature size of the plant. For instance, while a young tomato plant may look as if it will fit into a small pot, the mature plant may be 6 feet or more in height. You'll need a big container to hold a plant that size. A large 20-inch pot or a half-barrel works well, as do two or three stacked car tires. Tires also work well for potatoes, which need depth to grow. Start out by planting them in one tire. As they grow, add additional tires, filling them with a mixture of straw and soil. You'll eventually have a tower four or five tires tall. You may wish to start with a larger tire on the bottom to lend stability as the tower grows along with the potatoes. With any containers used, ensure that they are stable and won't topple over if a child leans on them to smell a flower or pick a vegetable.

One of the disadvantages of containers is that the soil dries out much more rapidly than with other kinds of gardens. In very

7-11-00

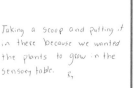

Taking a scoop and putting it in there because we wanted the plants to grow in the sensory table. R.

We put water absorbing crystals in water and watched them grow.

hot weather, small containers may need watering twice a day. We recommend adding soil polymers to the soil to increase the water retention. These are available under a number of brand names at nurseries and garden centers. They're small crystals that absorb water and increase dramatically in size. Because of this fascinating ability, they make a terrific science experiment, if closely supervised by a teacher. (You don't want children to swallow these, as they do absorb huge amounts of water. Supervision is essential. If you have children who can't resist putting things in their mouths, you might want to add the polymers to the soil yourself when the children are not present.) In addition to using the soil polymers, you should consider adding a mulch, such as wood chips or small pebbles, to containers to slow down evaporation. Remember that the larger the containers you use, the less you will have to worry about the plants drying out.

If you need to use containers and have no way of watering over long weekends, consider installing a simple irrigation system. Drip water systems are available at most discount stores, as well as at garden centers and are surprisingly easy to set up. These can be attached, using a hose, to a timer that will regulate the watering over the weekend for you.

Most experts recommend using a potting mix for containers. You can buy potting mix already made at any garden center or you can make your own. We have a recipe for a mix in chapter 8, but you'll find many recipes in garden books and magazines. If you buy your potting mix, avoid the kind with fertilizer mixed in, as it should not be handled by children. With either premixed or your own mix, add the soil polymers, following the directions on the container. If you are planting a large container, such as a boat or swimming pool, you can use the same kind of mix you would use for a raised bed.

When planting a container, place pieces of broken terra-cotta pots, large chunks of gravel, or styrofoam packing peanuts in the bottom of the container before adding the soil mix. This will increase the effectiveness of the drainage. Fill the container to about 1 inch from the top, so you'll have space for watering. If the container is large, place it in the location where it will remain before adding the soil mix and plants. If the location of your container garden is on a patio, consider that water will run onto the surface underneath. So you may want to place the container away from an entrance or popular path.

## Indoor Gardens

Teachers should consider an indoor garden if an outdoor garden seems to present too many obstacles. Although the experience will be different from that of studying an outdoor garden ecosystem, it can be rewarding for the children to study plants in any environment. One advantage of indoor gardening is that you can grow plants in any season. This may be of particular benefit to preschool programs that are on a nine-month calendar or in very cold climates.

Indoor gardens are really container gardens, and the previous instructions for planting containers apply to them as well. The exception is that you will need to provide trays to catch the water runoff. Trays made specifically for this purpose are available in the garden section of most discount stores, but you can improvise and use any flat object with a lip that will hold the container.

The major difficulty in building an indoor garden is providing enough light for the plants. If you have sunny windows, you may be able to grow some herbs and flowers on the windowsill. However, if you are going to be gardening on a larger scale, you will need to devise an indoor lighting system, using fluorescent lights. If you choose to go this route, we recommend that you consult the book *Grow Lab: A Complete Guide to Gardening in the Classroom* (National Gardening Association 1988). This book contains illustrated instructions for building an extensive lighting system, which will sustain a number of plants. *Grow Lab* was written specifically for teachers who want to garden in the classroom and includes much information that will be helpful in establishing an indoor garden.

## Plant Selection

One of the most important parts of the gardening process is selecting the plants you will grow. Children should be actively involved in choosing which plants to include in the garden. However, it helps if the adult has a basic understanding of plant hardiness and how plants are affected by climate. You will need to consider several factors before making your plant selections. These include the climate in which you live, whether you want an annual or perennial garden, and whether to start with seeds or purchase transplants.

## Annuals or Perennials

First consider whether you want to grow annuals or perennials. Annuals are plants that grow for only one season, while perennials come back year after year. Many gardeners prefer annual flowers because they tend to bloom continuously throughout the season, providing constant color to the garden, while most perennials have a shorter blooming season. Another advantage of annuals is that you can change your garden easily every year. The old plants die off, leaving space to put in new ones in the spring.

Perennials, however, have the advantage of lasting. Though they cost more to buy initially, in the long run you'll spend less money. Not only that, but they multiply. By dividing your plants, you can make new ones to plant or to share with friends. Perennials take less time because you don't have to plant them every year. However, to maintain their health, you will need to divide them every two or three years.

You may choose to plant only annuals or only perennials in your garden. We have two garden areas that are planted only with annuals. These spaces change each year. In one we plant different vegetables each spring. The other has been a North American garden, an Asian garden, and home for a sunflower house. We like the variety these gardens offer.

Our other gardens combine perennials with annuals. Since we have a large space to plant, we appreciate having plants that come back every year. They make less work for us in

the spring and save us money since we don't have to keep buying new plants. We add annuals to add color and interest to these areas.

Garden catalogs and nurseries generally separate annual and perennial plants, so it's easy to learn which is which. Some plants are annual in cold climates and perennial in warmer climates, so if you live in a warm area, you may have more perennials to choose from. In our area, some plants will come back the next year if we have a mild winter, but will die if we have a severe cold snap. Your local experts are the best people to guide you as you determine what plants are perennial in your area.

## Climate

The climate refers to the prevailing weather conditions for a particular region. Climate affects planting and harvesting times, as well as plant selection. You probably already have a good idea of what your climate is from having lived there, but you will now need to think about how your climate affects the plants in your area. You'll want to consider the average high and low temperatures for summer and winter, the general wind direction, and average yearly rainfall.

We live in a temperate climate with moderately cold winters and hot summers, so most of our suggestions are based on having a garden that experiences changes throughout the seasons. In this book, we've included some lists of plants for specific types of gardens and some sample garden designs. These plants do well in our climate and will grow in most temperate climates. However, if you live in the desert or in a tropical area, you'll need to take this into consideration and consult a local plant expert about plant choices.

## How to Make Hollyhock Dolls

To make hollyhock dolls, you will need a hollyhock bloom that is in full flower for the skirt and a bud for the head. When you pick the flower, be sure to include about ½ inch of the stem. Set the flower aside while you select and prepare the bud. Choose a bud that is just beginning to open up and is showing some color. Carefully remove the green covering from the bud. Pull the stem and attached green off the bud. Where the stem was, there should be a small hole. You can enlarge this with a small stick. Now retrieve the flower. Place the hole of the bud on top of the stem of the flower and you will have your doll.

## Temperature

Temperature affects the length of the growing season. If you don't already know, find out the typical dates for the last and first frosts of the year in your area. These dates determine what plants can be grown, as well as when you can safely plant them. You'll also need to find out what zone your area is in, based on the United States Department of Agriculture Plant Hardiness Map, which reflects the average low temperature for the area. This map is available in almost every garden catalog, and you should also be able to find out your zone by consulting your local nursery. When buying seeds or plants from catalogs, be sure to check for the zone in which the plants will grow. Most catalogs will include this information in the plant listing. Nurseries and garden centers usually sell plants appropriate to the zone in which they are located. Note that some plants that are perennials in warmer climates may still be grown as annuals in cold climates.

The best resource for finding out what plants will do well in your area is local gardeners and gardening experts. Select a variety of plants that will provide diversity to your garden. Think about what you can do with the plants that will maintain the children's interest. For instance, flowers are beautiful to look at and some varieties are edible. By including edible flowers, you increase the appeal of your garden. Herbs can be dried or can be used for cooking and making such things as teas, flavored vinegars, and potpourri. In addition, the flowers of many herbs are attractive and can be used for decoration as well as cooking.

Some plants provide materials for future activities. We enjoy planting gourds, not only because they grow abundantly and cover our entire fence and trellis house, but because the gourds they produce can be used for making birdhouses and birdfeeders. Job's tears is a fun plant that produces beadlike seeds that children can string. Hollyhocks can be used to make hollyhock dolls, and snapdragons draw a child's interest because they can be manipulated to snap open and shut. Sunflowers can be planted in a circle or rectangle so they will eventually grow into the walls of a house or a fort. Vegetables are necessary if you want to involve the children in cooking activities.

One book that will be helpful to many teachers is *Plants for Play* (Moore 1993). Moore includes lists of plants that can be selected for fragrance, texture, wind effects, hiding places, play props, and many other attributes. An excellent source for learning about individual vegetables and herbs is *The Children's Kitchen Garden: A Book of Gardening, Cooking, and Learning* (Brennan and Brennan 1997). This book gives specific information about a large number of plants, including planting and harvesting recommendations, and includes a number of recipes.

The size of your garden and your theme, if you choose to have one, will help you determine your final plant choices. Consider spacing requirements as you make your final selection. These are available on seed packets or on the labels of live plants. If in doubt, ask.

If you live in an area where the winters are severe and the growing season is short, choose plants that either survive deep cold or that have a short growing season. Hot temperatures can be as limiting as cold temperatures since some plants are not heat tolerant. If you're not sure if a plant will do well, consult your local nursery. Most nurseries offer plants that do well in the area in which they are located. For that reason, local nurseries are a better place to buy plants than are garden companies located far away.

## Plants to Avoid

There are some plants you'll definitely want to avoid. These include plants that require a great deal of maintenance, such as most hybrid tea roses, which need to be sprayed regularly to prevent disease. In addition, some plants need to be placed carefully. If you plant a less fussy rosebush, a barberry, or any other plant with thorns, be sure to put it in an area where children are not likely to fall into it during their normal play. Thorns can cause a great deal of damage and emotional distress.

You also need to avoid plants that are toxic. We've included a list of poisonous plants in appendix 6, but this is only a partial guide. If you are unsure about the safety of a plant, call your local Poison Control Center. They have the most current information and are very helpful. Another good reference is *Plants for Play* (Moore 1993). Moore argues that not all poisonous plants need to be banned from school gardens. In fact, he stresses that children need to learn about poisonous plants, as they will come across them in their lives and need to be able to identify them and understand the dangers involved. He suggests the schoolyard can be a place where, under careful supervision, children can learn about some toxic plants. Moore also points out that different poisonous plants have different levels of toxicity. The plants he lists are divided by level of toxicity: highly toxic, moderately toxic, and slightly toxic. Highly toxic plants, such as castor beans, belladonna, and angel's trumpet can cause serious illness or even death if ingested. Moderately toxic plants, such as foxglove, English ivy, and columbine can cause illness when ingested or serious contact dermatitis if touched. Slightly toxic plants, such as bleeding heart and buttercups, might cause mild illness or contact dermatitis.

Consider the level of toxicity of the plant and the age and maturity of your children, as well as the educational value of the plant, when deciding whether you want to include it in your garden. You may also need to alter your plant selection if you have children with serious allergies. In addition, think about what part of the plant is toxic and how likely children are to come in contact with that part. You will want to be extremely cautious if you have children who are still prone to putting objects in their mouths. Avoid all toxic plants if infants and toddlers have access to an area, as well as plants with small berries or seeds that infants and toddlers might choke on. Above all, be sure that any staff or volunteers who are supervising children are well aware of any plants that might cause problems. Also, be sure to keep the number of the closest Poison Control Center next to the phone, in case of emergency. We also keep a poison control kit, containing syrup of ipecac and activated charcoal, in our medicine cabinet in case we need it.

## Seeds or Transplants?

Before the planting season arrives, you'll need to start thinking about whether you want to grow your own plants from seed or purchase plants ready to transplant into your garden. The teacher in you may think that planting seeds is the way to go if you want children to have the full experience of seeing how plants develop, and you would be right to a point. Certainly the experience of growing plants from seed will be fascinating for your children. Some plants grow easily from seed, and some plants are only available to you if you grow them yourself. Others need to be directly seeded because they do not transplant well. However, some plants are difficult to grow from seed and are most practically purchased as transplants. Also, the space available in many classrooms limits the number of seedlings that can be sustained during the late winter. We suggest that you consider using both methods. Grow some of the easier seeds in the classroom in the late winter and also use some transplants that have been purchased or donated.

We were fortunate that we were able to use a campus greenhouse to grow many of our plants, and we were able to entice volunteers to monitor and care for the plants in the greenhouse. Check around to see if there is greenhouse space available in your area. Since we were able to get much of our seed donated by mail-order companies, growing the seeds ourselves saved us a lot of money.

## Kid Tip

While you are waiting for seedlings to erupt, fill a sensory table or large tub with damp potting soil. (Be sure not to use soil that has fertilizer added to it. Look for plain, unadulterated potting mix.) As you plant seeds, add some to this mixture. As the seedlings that you plan to transplant grow undisturbed, the children can closely monitor the changes in the seeds in the sensory table.

## Growing Plants from Seed

If you plan to grow plants from seed, consider where you will get your seed. Seeds are available at many discount stores and garden centers, but you will have a better and often healthier selection if you order from catalogs. (A list of seed companies is in appendix 3.) You may be able to obtain donations of seeds from local merchants or mail-order companies. We recommend that you purchase seeds packaged for the year you are planting them. Look on the seed package to determine if they are the current year's supply. Seeds from previous years may germinate, but the success rate increases, as do the chances of a healthy plant, with fresher, properly stored seeds. If you do store seeds from year to year, be sure they are stored in a cool, dry space and are labeled for identification.

If you are going to grow seeds yourself, check the package to see whether they should be started indoors first or directly seeded into the garden. With those that need to be planted inside, you'll want to start early so that they'll be ready to plant in your garden by your frost-free date. Each packet of seeds tells how far ahead of time you should plant the seeds, and this varies depending on the plant. You'll need to determine your frost-free date and then count backward to come up with the right day to plant. For instance, the date after which we are usually frost-free in southern Illinois is April 15. If seeds take six weeks from planting time to mature, we would need to plant them the first week of March. Since different seeds need different lengths of time to develop, you will need to come up with a timetable for planting. (You can even use a large calendar and attach seed packets to the dates on which you plan to plant.) This can be fun in a classroom, as you will have many planting opportunities and seedlings will be springing up over a period of time. This helps sustain the children's interest as they wait for the actual planting time to come.

There are many methods that can be used to start seeds. You can purchase flats or peat pots intended for starting seeds, but you can also start seeds in milk cartons, egg cartons, or other used containers. If you reuse containers, be sure to disinfect them with a bleach-water solution. And no matter what type of container you use, buy new, sterile seed-starter mix. Your mix and containers must be free of bacteria if you are to have healthy plants.

Provide the proper amount of water to new seedlings. They need to be kept slightly moist, but too much water encourages fungus and root rot. If new seedlings start falling over and dying, you likely have a fungus that causes what is called "damping off," which must be avoided as it spreads to other young plants and can mean death for your seed-starting efforts. Our experiences with growing seeds in the classroom have taught us that children often overwater and that it is also difficult to keep seedlings moist over weekends. Because of this, we often use a seed-starting system that transfers water to the soil by means of a capillary mat, which is submerged in water at one end. This ensures that the soil remains consistently moist, even when we are gone. Children still have the experience of watering the seedlings by filling

7-11-00

We put the beans in there.
Ry

We put some seeds in the plaster. Alex did it too. Lexi did it too.

We planted beans in plaster to see if they would be strong enough to break the plaster. They did.

The beans swelled up and broke the plaster before they sprouted. Next time we'll plant them deeper.

the reservoir. These systems are available through nurseries or from The Gardener's Supply Company. (See appendix 3 for contact information.)

For best results with seeds started indoors, use fluorescent lights to help the plants grow. It's easy and surprisingly inexpensive to set up a lighting system. A 48-inch florescent light fixture can often be bought for under $10, and bulbs for such fixtures are reasonably priced. You can buy special plant bulbs, but these are more expensive and not necessary. Most experts suggest that you use one cool bulb and one warm bulb in a two-light fixture to provide an appropriate light-range for plants. Use lightweight chain to suspend the light fixture so you can change its height to keep it about 3 inches above the plants as they grow. A good source for information on growing plants inside is *Grow Lab: A Complete Guide to Gardening in the Classroom* (NGA 1988).

## Selecting Transplants

Flats of transplants can be purchased from nurseries, garden centers, discount stores, roadside stands, and even grocery stores. An incredible selection is available in early spring, and sometimes it seems impossible to go to a store that doesn't have plants for sale. Most plants will be

healthy and ready to grow if you get them soon after they arrive at the store. However, some stores have better strategies for caring for plants than others. Some seem to take the tactic of buying the plants, selling what they can, and letting the rest die. Therefore, if you get to the store early, you can get some real bargains. But if you wait, you might find mostly sick, wilting plants.

Look for healthy plants with bright, firm leaves. Feel free to pull one out of the pack to examine the roots. The root ball should simply lift out of the tray. The roots should be white and healthy looking. The soil should be moist if they are being well cared for. Avoid plants with roots that look as if they might be rotting.

Avoid plants in full flower or with vegetables already developing. If they are already blooming strongly, they won't transplant as well. You want small, compact, healthy plants, perhaps with buds starting to develop. Such plants should perform well for you.

Don't purchase the plant if it looks distressed, even if the price is reduced. Chances are it won't do well, and it could carry a disease that will affect the rest of your garden. Healthy transplants are critical in getting your garden off to a good start.

# References

Brennan, Georgeanne, and Ethel Brennan. 1997. *The children's kitchen garden: A book of gardening, cooking, and learning.* Berkeley, Calif.: Ten Speed Press.

Moore, Robin C. 1993. *Plants for play.* Berkeley, Calif.: MIG Communications.

National Gardening Association (NGA). 1988. *Grow lab: A complete guide to gardening in the classroom.* South Burlington, Vt.: National Gardening Association.

# 5

# Working with Children in the Garden

## Planting the Garden

Once you have prepared your garden beds and obtained your seeds and transplants, it's time for you to plant your garden. Be sure to wait until your area is free of frost or you will risk losing all your plants. You will need to plan carefully for the actual planting of the garden, and your strategy will differ depending on the size of your garden and the types of plants you are including.

As you think about how you will plant the garden, consider what you will do to ensure that the children feel ownership for the garden. If a number of adults come in and take control, children will likely miss out on much of the planting process. If they are to perceive the garden as their own, you will want to include them in the planting as much as possible.

A small, simple garden with only flowers and vegetables can be planted over a period of a few days or a week, a few plants at a time. This technique works well as it gives teachers an opportunity to work with small groups of children. The teacher can provide a rich experience as children examine the roots of the transplants and compare the size, shape, and texture of seeds. Often there is a temptation to plant the entire garden at once, but the process of spending time with children should not be sacrificed for the benefit of getting everything in the ground.

If you are gardening on a larger scale or if you will be doing heavy work, such as moving large boulders, installing stepping-stones, or planting shrubs or trees, you may need to arrange a more organized event. When we first planted our garden, we had the assistance of a college class that came to help us do the heavy labor and get the plants in the ground, so we did all the planting in one day. While this certainly got the garden planted, we found that sometimes the children were left out in the hurry to get all the plants in. In subsequent years we have avoided this problem by taking a more leisurely approach to planting the garden. We still have a class of college students come and help us, but now we have them concentrate on doing the heavy labor or working one-on-one with our children in planting. We save some plants to be planted throughout the next week or two.

If you decide to involve a large number of people, think clearly what you want their role to be and communicate this to them. Devise a plan that will be easy for them to follow. All hard construction, such as building retaining walls, raised beds, fences, paths, trellises, and play-houses, or moving large boulders should be completed before planting. If your work crew is going to perform any of this work, have those who will be involved come early so that it will be finished before the actual planting begins. If the work is extensive, it will need to be done prior to the planting day.

While the children will not be able to participate in this heavy labor, they will enjoy watching and asking questions as others do the work. Our children were fascinated when Sara's husband, Charles, came in with his rototiller to prepare the soil in one bed. After watching him work, they decided to include a photograph of him tilling in their garden journal.

Once the construction is complete and the planting area is prepared, you'll be ready to plant. Well before your planting day, prepare markers or flags with the names of the plants or seeds you will be planting. Before anyone begins to plant, place these in your garden in the exact place you want the plant or seed to go. Then take the actual seeds or plants and place them as close as possible to the space where they will go, without blocking the planting area.

Next, get all your tools ready. We use hand tools with our children. Our experience has shown us that preschoolers and kindergarteners often have difficulty handling long-handled tools safely. There is an incredible urge to swing hoes up over the shoulder, and this can be disastrous if other children are standing behind when it happens. After a few nerve-wracking experiences, we started using hand trowels and cultivators. Since the soil in our garden is easy to work, these are sufficient.

If you have older children (second or third graders, for example), you might want to experiment with long-handled tools for bigger jobs, but carefully instruct the children in their use and closely monitor them.

In addition to trowels, we also keep a large supply of gloves in both adult and child sizes. Many adults prefer to wear gloves, and we like to give children the same option. Children's garden gloves are easily obtainable at discount stores and garden centers.

Explain the procedure for planting to teachers and volunteers who are helping. Be sure they understand how to plant the seeds or transplants they will be dealing with. This won't be a problem if you have experienced gardeners, but novices will need basic information such as the following:

✿ Some seeds are broadcast over a general area and some are planted in holes. Read the package directions carefully to find out how to plant each type of seed.

✿ Most seeds need to be planted at a depth no greater than two or three times their size. If planted deeper, they may not come up. Again, seed packages should give clear directions about planting depth. Children may be tempted to dig deep holes and bury seeds too well. They will need assistance in planting to avoid this.

✿ Care is necessary to remove transplants from their packaging. Sometimes the best way to do this is to gently squeeze the container around the roots. As much as possible, avoid pulling on the stems of plants, as they are very fragile. If you simply pull on the plant to remove it, you run the risk of breaking it apart. Special care should be taken in showing children how to do this.

✿ If plants were grown in biodegradable pots, such as peat pots, they can be planted directly into the ground without being removed from the pot. If the pot is formed of peat, be careful that it is entirely covered with soil or it may dry out easily. You may want to tear off the top part of the pot if it protrudes above the soil level, since the soil should come to the same level it did in the original pot.

✿ Dig holes slightly larger that the root ball of the plant. (The root ball includes the roots of the plant and the surrounding soil.) Plant the transplants so that they will rest at the same soil level as they did in their original containers.

✿ Before planting transplants, gently tease the roots apart at the bottom. (Children enjoy doing this.) This helps the roots grow deep into the ground, rather than continuing to grow around in a circle, as they may have done in their original container.

✿ Once the plant is in the ground, gently pat the soil around it to stabilize it. If you are planting shrubs or trees, get specific planting instructions for them when you make your purchase. You'll probably want to plant these larger plants first.

Once you have given instructions to your assistants, assign children to specific adults. Since this may be the first day the children have actually worked in the garden, they are apt to be enthusiastic so we find it best to keep groups small. Sometimes we have been able to assign each child to a single adult, but this is not always possible. Two preschool-age children per adult is ideal, and four children is workable if the adult is experienced working with groups of children. Keep your groups small and let children go in shifts rather than overburdening a volunteer with more children than can be easily handled.

Once all the plants are in the ground, you may want to mulch, although it is not necessary to do this right away. If you choose to mulch, instructions on mulching are included later in this chapter. You will certainly need to water the garden thoroughly as soon as you are finished planting. This is crucial for young transplants as well as for seeds, which need moisture in order to germinate. Be sure that the garden remains moist over the next few days to ensure germination and allow plants to establish themselves in their new environment.

## Every Day in the Garden

Once you've built and planted your garden, you're well into your garden project. Now you begin the best times of all, as your garden becomes a part of every school day. The next sections cover

- How to supervise children in the garden
- How to maintain your garden
- How to take advantage of the creatures that inhabit and visit your garden
- How to get rid of undesirable creatures in your garden, if desired
- Ideas for harvesting plants and seeds

## Supervising Children in the Garden

Many garden activities at our school occur informally during the time children are playing on the playground, where they have access to about half of the garden. However, sometimes more formal activities take place that require closer attention from an adult. Examples of these activities include planting, weeding, deadheading, and harvesting. Supervising a large number of children in these activities is difficult, especially if we have to go to the area of the garden that is outside the playground fence. We try to limit the number of children involved in these activities, so that an adult is able to keep a close eye on what the children are doing and provide appropriate guidance. For our preschoolers, the optimal number of children seems to be four or five, depending on their ages. Since few programs have ratios of one adult to four or five children, it may be helpful to find volunteers to assist during these times. Parents are often happy to help. (We have had more parents volunteer to help with gardening than any other activity.) Many communities have garden clubs whose members would jump at the chance to involve children in their favorite hobby. And if you are near a university, you might be

able to recruit student volunteers. Many fraternities and sororities are looking for service work. All you have to do is ask.

Think about dividing children into pairs and assigning specific tasks to each pair. By providing children with partners, you will also set the stage for negotiation and problem solving, as children learn to cooperate to accomplish goals.

When you're working in the garden with children, inevitably someone is going to make a mistake. Sometimes a child trying to pick a flower will pull up the whole plant. Or a child will pull up a cherished plant, mistaking it for a weed. Sara had a hard time holding her tongue the day she learned that a volunteer, who was helping the children weed, had pulled up the Job's tears she had carefully nurtured from seeds. But learn to take such actions in stride. Sometimes the plant can be placed back in the ground with little harm done. Even if the plant is past saving, the damage done to it is less than the damage you could do by overreacting. Remember that the garden project is a learning experience. One thing children will learn is that sometimes when you pull a plant up, roots and all, it dies.

Since part of our garden is located on our playground, the children have access to this section any time they are outside. We've learned that we need to watch children carefully, and if they move into the garden area, we are careful to position a teacher nearby. Because children are natural explorers, they will often be tempted to pick unripe vegetables or flowers that are being saved for a special activity. This can be disappointing to other children when the group has made plans for harvesting. With a teacher nearby, watching and redirecting, problems are less likely to occur. It is also more likely that the teacher will be able to optimize teachable moments, since she will be more aware of the children's interests.

Since children do like to dig and explore, it helps to give them some space where they can do this without damaging the plants in the main garden. We've set aside a small plot where children can dig and plant seeds, and plant and dig up plants, as much as they like. This area is labeled with a sign that says, "Digging Area." A crate with trowels and gardening gloves is kept there so children don't need to ask a teacher for tools. You might be able to pick up plants for this area by asking a store with a garden center to let you go through plants they plan to discard every so often. You can often find a few healthy plants among the dying.

Some areas of a garden may require props if the children are to get the most out of them. For instance, we built a trellis house, which grows over with vines every summer. We want children to get the feeling of being inside this wonderful environment, where gourds hang down from overhead and vines creep over the windows. However, an empty house has limited appeal. By allowing the children to bring boards and crates inside and to build tables and chairs with them, we opened up many opportunities for dramatic play. One year, the children didn't seem to be moving into the house to play at all, so we placed a table and chairs inside and added dishes. Immediately children began to play inside the trellis house. After this, we periodically changed the materials inside to keep the children interested and motivated.

We had a similar situation the year we built our first sunflower house. At first, the children didn't seem to notice the open area inside. By adding a blanket and books, we were able to show children the possibilities of this area. Soon they were inside, snuggling up with a teacher or a friend as they read together. By varying the materials, we were able to expand the interest in the sunflower house. From these experiences we learned that if the children are not as interested in the garden as we would like them to be, we needed to modify the environment to introduce new forms of play.

## Maintaining the Garden

Once your planting is finished, you should devise a system for maintaining the garden. You'll need to be certain that plants receive the moisture they need and that weeds are kept in check if you want your plants to flourish. You may also need to fertilize the garden to be sure plants receive plenty of nutrients. If you want flowers to continue to develop as long as possible, you need to deadhead (cut away old flowers). In addition, think about ways to help staff and volunteers identify the plants.

## Mulching

Mulching the garden is one of the wisest steps you can take to retain moisture in the garden and reduce the weed population. Many types of mulch are available. In selecting one, you'll need to consider your budget, as well as appearance. Also, in some regions certain mulches are readily available; other mulches might be difficult to find. You may want to use several mulches so children can observe and compare the effectiveness of each. One of the most common mulches is bark or wood chips. You can purchase these by the bag at garden centers and discount stores, but it is more economical to buy in quantity from a nursery. Beware of wood chips donated by a utility company. These can contain substances—such as herbicides, insecticides, or poison ivy—that you don't want in your garden. Sometimes sheets of black plastic or landscape fabric are used as mulch, but be aware that water will not penetrate the plastic. A fun mulch to try is cocoa hulls. They're rather expensive in our area, but have the advantage of smelling like chocolate. Less expensive mulches include grass clippings, newspaper, straw, leaves, pine needles, and sawdust.

Mulching is always an appealing experience for our children. We use shredded bark mulch, which the university grounds staff dump in a large pile by our garden. The children fill child-size wheelbarrows with the mulch and wheel it to the part of the garden where they will be working. Amazingly, some children will spend a couple of hours on this task. Supervise carefully when children are applying mulch because it is easy to inadvertently bury tender young plants. With annuals, leave a bit of space between the mulch and the plant, since the damp mulch could cause the foliage to rot. However, you can mulch up close to perennials and shrubs.

## Weeding and Watering

Set up a schedule for watering and weeding. We water once a week, unless it rains. Depending on your climate, you may need to water more or less. Find out what is recommended for your area. Since we want to give plants about an inch of water a week, we use a rain gauge to check rainfall. If we get an inch of rain over a week's time, we don't water. By monitoring the rain gauge, the children gain an understanding of how we need to supplement Mother Nature in caring for our garden.

The biggest chore in gardening is the weeding. You can keep your garden under control if you make this a weekly event. This is why you need to keep your garden a manageable size. If your garden is small, you may be able to keep the children interested long enough to weed your garden on a regular basis. However, because of the size of our garden, we constantly struggle with weeds. Each year we come up with a new plan for controlling them, and honestly, we haven't found a perfect solution yet. Our children do eagerly weed throughout much of the summer. They quickly learn to identify weeds and remove them, and we've had many meaningful learning experiences counting and measuring weeds.

However, because of the size of our garden, the children cannot be expected to do all the weeding. At times we have had college students who were willing help us with the weeding over the summer. Other times, we have had small groups of people come in and weed. Perhaps you could select a weekly weeding day and invite parents and/or community gardeners to join you for the fun.

We pull most of our weeds by hand. This is easier if the ground is damp, so water the day before you weed. We like pulling weeds because the weeds are less likely to come back if they are pulled, and it also gives us an opportunity to examine the different root systems of plants with the children. However, if you have large areas of weeds, using a hoe is much quicker. If you are going to hoe, it is safer for the plants and the children if an adult does the work. If you let children hoe, monitor them closely.

## Feeding Your Plants

If you start out your garden with rich compost, it may do well the first year without any additional fertilizer. However, for the healthiest plants, especially after the first year, you'll want to provide nutrients to your garden. If you garden in containers, you need to feed your plants, as repeated watering washes nutrients out of the pot. Many good fertilizers are available and your choice will depend on the age of the children and how you use the fertilizer.

For containers, we prefer to add some slow-release fertilizer to the soil when we plant. These fertilizers, which feed plants by dissolving slowly over a period of four to six months, need to be used carefully around children, since they usually come in a pellet form that may be attractive to those who are still putting objects in their mouths. However, when they are mixed with the soil in containers, children are not likely to come in contact with them, and they provide consistent food where other fertilizers are washed out of the container. If you are concerned that the children may put pellets in their mouths, either do not use them or bury them deep in the pots in a single layer, rather than dispersing them throughout the soil. We do not use slow-release fertilizer in the garden, where children will be digging.

For the children's use we prefer natural, organic fertilizers, since they pose less risk for children than chemical fertilizers. You have many choices here, such as blood meal, bonemeal, seasoned manure, cottonseed meal, fish meal, and fish emulsion fertilizer. While many adults balk at the disagreeable smell of fish emulsion fertilizer, children seem to have a special affinity for anything adults find disgusting. They also enjoy using substances such as manure, which appeal to their sense of humor. If you use manure, you need to make sure it is well-aged or it can burn the plants and kill them. You might also want to involve children in making manure or alfalfa tea that can be used to feed plants. We've included recipes for these in chapter 8.

If you use organic fertilizers, you need to be aware that they take longer to break down and become available to the plants, so they are not a quick fix. If you need something that will give plants an immediate boost, water-soluble fertilizers work well. Be cautious in using these with children. (We would not use these at all in the presence of infants and toddlers, since they make a blue liquid that a young child might want to drink. If your children are this young, feed the plants when they are not around.) You can mix the fertilizer in a watering can and carefully supervise the children as they distribute the food, or you can use a hose-end sprayer for larger areas. In either case, be sure any children you involve in this activity are responsible and closely monitored.

## Deadheading

If you want your flowers to keep blooming throughout the season, you'll need to remove the spent flowers. Herbs will quit producing as well, if their flowers are allowed to go to seed. Once the flower of a plant dies, the plant begins to make seeds in order to reproduce. Seed production is a signal to the plant to quit making flowers. You can interrupt this signal by removing the flower so the plant will make more flowers in its determined effort to reproduce. This process is called "deadheading."

There are many theories about the best way to deadhead, but for your purposes the process is simple. Simply cut the flower off. We try to cut flowers in time to use them for decoration or activities in the classroom, but the flowers often bloom faster than we can work. Sometimes we take the children out with scissors and let them cut to their hearts' content. If you have mums in your garden, you'll want to cut them back a couple of times over the summer *before* they bloom so you'll have compact, healthy blooms in the fall. If stems are very tough, children's scissors might not be sufficient for cutting. In this case, we take pruning shears and either deadhead ourselves or closely supervise one child at a time with the shears.

## Labeling

Label plants if you have a number of people spending time in a garden. While you may have a clear idea of what you planted and where you put it, other visitors to the garden might have some trouble identifying what plant is which. We've experimented with a number of labels over the years and found that most have both positive and negative attributes. Think about what is most important to you. Do you want labels that are easy to read, that will last, or that the children can make?

There are many ways to make labels. For instance, children can cover seed packets with clear Con-Tact paper and attach them to a stick. They can also use Popsicle sticks or other pieces of wood to make labels, writing the name of the plant with a marker. Homemade labels are great for helping children feel ownership of the garden. However, they often do not last long if you experience a great deal of wet weather.

Plant markers are also available for purchase. The least expensive kind are simple plastic sticks with pointed ends that you push into the ground. We haven't found these to be effective for our use, since the name of the plant is sideways once the marker is in the ground and children have to turn their heads to read them. This is confusing for children who are just learning to read. We use these to label seed trays, but we do not use them in the garden. Some of the best moderate-priced markers are zinc plates on wires that are pushed into the ground. We don't use these in the part of the garden that is accessible to the children, since we worry that the wire could injure a child. However, we do use them in the part of the garden that is outside the fence, since children are always closely supervised in this area. The markers we have used inside the fence most recently are plastic, with space to write horizontally at the top. These are somewhat expensive and the writing must be small, since we can only afford the smallest markers, but they are easy to read.

Experiment with different types of markers to see what works for you. Let children work with a variety of materials to come up with their own plant labels. They may surprise you with some of their ideas.

## Garden Creatures

No matter how small your garden, you will find that it attracts animals. These may be minuscule insects and other bugs or mammals, such as rabbits, squirrels, chipmunks, and deer. One question you'll have to ask is whether these animals are friend or foe—a more complex question than it seems at first glance. For instance, some gardeners spend many hours devising methods to keep squirrels out of their gardens and birdfeeders. Indeed, squirrels will steal from the garden and they will eat food intended for our feathered friends. But in the children's garden they offer much opportunity for study. One fascinating experience occurred when a

mother squirrel built her nest in the hollow of a tree just a few feet outside our playground fence. The children and teachers enjoyed following the growth of the two babies and observing their antics as they chased each other around the trunk of the tree. We would not have traded this experience for a better harvest or more food for the birds. In fact, our campus is so heavily populated with squirrels that it would be impossible to discourage them from inhabiting our playground, even if we didn't have a garden. We've learned to live with them and to grow a little more so there will be enough to share. Establishing such an attitude toward wildlife is an important part of managing a garden when children are involved. Advantage must always be weighed against disadvantage.

In addition, the safety of the children is of utmost importance. Chemical pesticides should never be used in an area that is to be inhabited by children. We've found that, by choosing hardy plants, we are able to maintain a healthy garden and pests are rarely so destructive that they completely kill a plant. In the cases where this is a problem, we use the opportunity as a learning experience and may decide to eliminate that plant from the garden the next year.

If you notice that something is damaging or stealing your crops, the first thing you should do is find out what is happening. Involve the children in the process. This is a good time to bring out their investigative skills. When you notice the problem, ask the children what they think might be causing it. Accept all their answers. Write them down so you can follow up with further investigation. Some steps you and the children can take to determine who the culprit is include the following:

🐝 Look at the plant carefully. Do you see any insects on it? Get out a magnifying glass. Now can you see anything? Shake the leaves over a piece of white paper and examine again with a magnifying glass. Very small creatures, such as spider mites, that aren't apparent on the leaf may be visible against the white paper. If you find something, consult a reference book or a gardening expert to help you identify it. Be sure to include the children in this process.

🐝 Take some time to observe if you can't find anything on the plant. Encourage the children to watch carefully while they are in or near the garden. They might spot a rabbit, bird, or other animal coming into the garden.

🐝 Do some research if you still can't figure out what is happening. You can start by looking through reference books, or you might want to involve the children in some active investigation. Children can start by interviewing their parents. Most schools will have some parents who have a lot of gardening experience and can come up with the answer. Another possibility is to call in a gardening expert. You can usually find someone through your extension service or at a garden center. If you can't get someone to come to you, take a piece of the damaged plant to a garden center for analysis.

Once you have determined what is damaging your plants, you'll need to decide what to do about it. The children should be instrumental in making this decision. Consider the following options:

✳ Leave it alone. Sometimes the damage is minimal or the culprit is so interesting that you don't really want to discourage it from coming to your garden.

✳ Research ways to deal with the pest. For instance, if birds are stealing from your garden, have the children interview family members to come up with ways to keep the birds out of the garden. Since there are many theories on how to keep birds away, the children will probably come up with a variety of ideas. (If you don't really want to keep the birds away, relax. Although many gardeners use scarecrows or models of owls or snakes to get rid of birds, these methods aren't terribly effective. If your birds aren't scared off by children running and yelling, it's doubtful they'll be bothered by scarecrows. Chances are you'll still have plenty of birds to study.)

✳ Decide on a safe way to tackle the problem if you decide you want to eliminate the pest. Avoid using any chemical pesticides. In chapter 8, we've included some safe recipes for sprays that can be used by children. Soap sprays are particularly effective, but applications need to be repeated on a regular basis. Our children have an undying enthusiasm for spraying plants with squirt bottles, so it hasn't been a problem to arrange for repeated sprayings. If your children are less interested, you can use the opportunity to inspect plants when they are not sprayed and compare them to when they are.

*green lacewing*

✳ Use insects to get rid of insects. Many people know that ladybugs eat aphids, and ladybug releases are becoming increasingly common. However, ladybugs are not the best insect predators. Other insects, such as green lacewings, have more voracious appetites. Beneficial insects are being used now, more than ever, in controlling garden pests, and can be purchased from a variety of sources. Some of these are listed in appendix 3. By introducing predators into the garden, you can help the children gain a concrete understanding of the food chain. *Good Bugs for Your Garden* (Starcher 1998) is a good reference book to help you learn more about beneficial insects.

✳ You may decide to remove the plant. This could be the best option if the plant is diseased and there is no cure for the disease or if the only cure would be dangerous for the children. If the disease poses no threat to the rest of your garden, you may also choose to leave the plant and let the children observe the progress of the disease.

> ## Plants that Deter Insects
> Some plants are believed to keep away insects. You might try planting the following among your other plants to see if they repel pests.
>
> asters
> chrysanthemums
> geraniums
> marigolds
> onions
> calendula

As you involve children in studying and making decisions about the garden ecosystem, they will begin to gain a greater understanding of the interdependence between the plants and animals. As a teacher, the more you learn about the animals you encounter, the more you will be able to foster the children's awareness. The following are descriptions of just a few creatures you may find in your garden. This information is included to give teachers an initial understanding. If you do encounter these animals, you will want to involve the children in further study. Reference books are valuable in this process, and in the appendices you will find a list of some excellent books about these creatures.

## The Good Guys
You will definitely want to invite some animals into your garden. When giving presentations, we have been surprised that adults sometimes have difficulty discriminating between beneficial

creatures and pests. Here are some insights into attracting and studying just a few of the animals that are helpful to the gardener.

### Worms

Worms are wonderful! Worms are great! Worms till the soil, bringing oxygen to the roots of plants. They eat organic matter and turn it into fertilizer. If you want to check the health of your soil, count your worms. The more worms you have, the better the soil is likely to be.

Worms are also great subjects for study. Give them a choice between a damp and a dry environment and watch them scurry over to the damp. Give them the opportunity and they will choose to be in the dark rather than the light. Later in this book, you'll find some experiments you can try with worms. Also, consider starting a worm composter. You can purchase worms by the pound, and they'll eat your leftover fruits and vegetables. The resultant castings can be put in your garden to help your plants grow. What other creature does so much?

Our favorite activity with earthworms is simple in design. We simply put worms out for the children to explore and make sure a teacher is available to guide their interactions with and observations of the worms. To do this, we use cafeteria trays, but any trays or pans with a lip will do. We put moist paper towels on the trays to prevent the worms from drying out and dying. (This is essential any time you take worms out of their environment for a period of time.) Then we put several worms on each tray. The worms are a virtual child-magnet. We've had children spend an entire hour exploring worms in this manner. (We also do this with pill bugs or roly-polys, which can be found under rocks or rotting wood in the garden or other natural areas.) In chapter 7 we have described some more sophisticated experiments.

### Bees

Bees are some of the most fascinating insects around. Most children know that bees make honey. Some people think they do this by collecting pollen. Actually, bees collect nectar from flowers to make honey. As they do this, they pick up pollen and carry it from flower to flower, performing the essential job of pollination. Bees are so essential to agriculture that farmers often pay beekeepers to keep bees on their farms or in their orchards. As common as bees are, many misconceptions exist. Help children understand the following:

⊛ The bees you see in the garden are worker bees. These are all females. The only job the male bees (drones) have is to mate with the queen bee, so they stay back at the hive.

⊛ Only female bees sting. The male bee has no stinger. (Therefore, if you've been singing "I'm Bringing Home a Baby Bumblebee" and including the words, "Ouch, *he* stung me," you are technically incorrect.)

⊛ Bees sting only if they are afraid. Bees die once they have stung, so they don't go around looking for opportunities to attack. Teach children how to behave properly around bees to avoid stings. Some adults are terrible role models for this. As soon as they see a bee, they start swinging their arms and flailing around. The message to the bee is clear: this person is trying to kill me. This is the likeliest way to be stung. Teach children to move slowly around bees. If children stand still or move with caution, the bees will not feel threatened and they will not sting. In fact, bees will often land on people and walk

around on them without posing a threat, so long as the person remains quiet. If you can teach yourself to remain calm around bees, you will be a great role model for children.

Some children are highly allergic to bee stings. If you have such a child in your program, you might want to avoid plants that draw a lot of bees. You will also need to work with the child's parents to develop a plan of action in case the child is stung.

## Ladybugs

Ladybugs, also known as ladybird beetles, are favored garden predators. Few children can resist picking up a ladybug and letting it crawl across their hands. These are gentle creatures, and their hearty appetite for that unwelcome garden pest, the aphid, makes them welcome visitors to the garden. Although they are often available from commercial suppliers, if you want ladybugs to stay in your garden, you'll have to be careful about introducing them. If you dampen the plants before releasing the ladybugs and choose a release time early in the morning or late in the day, they'll be more likely to stay. Also, be sure to place them at the base of plants actually infested with aphids, rather than simply letting them go anywhere. If they have food to eat, they'll be less likely to flee. Be sure to look up ladybugs in a reference book, so that you will be able to identify the larvae. Though not as attractive as the mature beetles, the larvae have more voracious appetites and are the key to maintaining a population of ladybugs in your garden.

## Praying Mantis

An impressive creature with bulging eyes and long legs, the praying mantis is often found in the garden. The name comes from the way the mantis positions its front legs, as though it is praying. The praying mantis is the only insect that can look over its shoulder, giving it a rather quizzical appearance. These insects are often hard to spot, as their protective coloration serves them well in the garden environment. They have big appetites and will eat even large insects, such as grasshoppers and bees. Their only drawback is that they're as likely to eat beneficial insects as they are pests.

If you don't have any praying mantises in your garden, you can purchase egg cases from commercial suppliers. To provide for closer observation by the children, these can be hatched inside. You'll need to do this in the early spring, usually late April or early May. (You can buy the egg cases earlier than this and refrigerate them until your area is frost-free.)

Place the egg case in a jar. Be sure to place a couple layers of cheesecloth or pantyhose over the top of the jar before you put on a lid with holes punched in it. The hatchlings are tiny and we've heard stories of them escaping through the holes in a jar lid. An egg case holds up to two hundred eggs, so this could result in more excitement than you want!

Release the nymphs soon after they hatch because they'll be hungry and newly hatched nymphs may eat each other if they don't have sufficient food. However, you may want to keep one nymph to observe indoors. It's likely you won't see the ones you release outside. They're very small and they may leave the area or be eaten by other predators. It takes five months for a nymph to grow to a full-size praying mantis.

# Discovering a Daddy Longlegs Spider

Trevor saw a daddy longlegs outside by the climber.  He tried to step on it, but Sara stopped him. She showed Trevor and Marquis how to hold the spider gently. They were a little frightened at first, but they became braver as they spent more time with the spider.

They dropped it a few times, as it tickled their hands and arms, but the spider was all right. They picked it up and tried again. After awhile, Trevor and Marquis put the daddy longlegs spider on a sunflower. The spider dropped to the ground and crawled away.

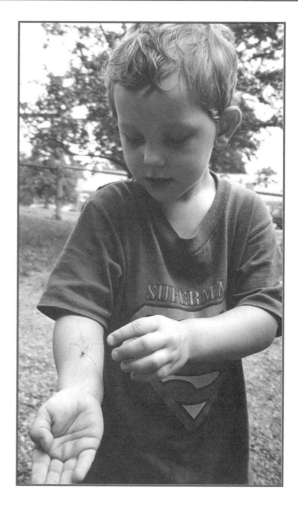

### Learning and Development
Marquis and Trevor are learning actively with their senses. They see the spider. They touch it. They feel it as it crawls on their arms. They are making discoveries through direct experience. They use language to discuss the experience, and later to add dictation to their photographs. Although their first instinct was to kill the spider, the teacher's intervention led them to investigate further, capturing their curiosity and invoking a sense of wonder. Finally, they respectfully returned the spider to a safe place.

### Spiders

Spiders are not only good garden predators, they are fascinating subjects for study. Their intricately designed webs are marvels of geometry, and their penchant for wrapping their prey with silk before feasting makes them especially engaging to young children. Be sure to let children know that spiders are not insects but arachnids. Children can learn to tell the difference by counting legs. Insects have six; arachnids have eight.

You should be cautious about handling spiders. While most poisonous varieties do not hang out in the garden, some spiders will bite when provoked, so most varieties are best observed without handling. The only exception we make to this rule is with daddy longlegs, which technically are arachnids, but not spiders. They are gentle, harmless, and easily identifiable.

If you let children hold a daddy longlegs, supervise closely, since their delicate legs are easily damaged. We require that children hold them with open hands only and return them immediately after examination to the place where they were found.

### Frogs and Toads

Frogs and toads are voracious eaters and will help keep down the insect and slug population in your garden. If you are lucky enough to have these amphibians near your garden, the children will enjoy capturing and studying them. Just be sure to release them at the end of the day at the same spot where they were found. You can make a home for a toad by partially burying a terra-cotta flowerpot on its side. If you plant a hosta or a daylily in front of the opening, the plant will provide extra protection for the toad.

### Snakes

That's right, snakes are good guys in the garden. One of the most maligned animals in history, the snake does more than its share of the work in keeping down the pest population, feeding on insects and small animals, such as mice and rats. Many adults react with panic when they see snakes, passing their prejudices and fears down to the next generation. Since young children don't come with preconceptions about these reptiles, an adult who can model respect and appreciation for snakes can go a long way in building positive attitudes.

Few species of snakes in the United States are poisonous, and these are not likely to be attracted to a garden in temperate regions such as ours. (Of course, if you should find yourself with a poisonous variety, call animal control to remove it immediately.) In addition, snakes are shy creatures and usually flee when they encounter humans. You may have to be more wary of snakes if you live in a region where poisonous snakes are common, such as rattlesnakes in the Southwest.

Still, if you are lucky enough to have a snake visit, use the opportunity for a learning experience. Let the children observe from a distance. If you absolutely feel the snake must go, under no circumstances should you kill it. Find someone who knows how to handle snakes and have her remove the snake humanely and relocate it. If you do this, the children will learn that all animals deserve respect.

## The Bad Guys

You'll have the opportunity to get to know a lot of insects and other bugs in the garden. Many of these will enjoy chomping the leaves of the plants you have so carefully nurtured. You will probably want to rid the garden of some of these pests. Some of them can be handpicked or simply washed off the plants with a strong stream of water. Others will need to be sprayed with a soap or other safe spray. You might even want to try using beneficial insects (see ladybugs and praying mantises, above) to control the population of damage-causing bugs. Listed below are some common garden pests.

### Aphids

Aphids are small, soft-bodied insects that feed on the sap of plants. They can often be found clustered around the buds and stems. Aphids can be white, black, or green. If you have them, you may notice deformed buds or flowers or stunted growth. Plants with aphids will be more susceptible to disease. The simplest form of control is washing them off the plant, but you may also choose to use a safe spray, such as a soap spray, to control them. Ladybugs and ladybug larvae like to eat aphids, so you also might want to bring some aphids and ladybugs into the classroom to observe.

*aphid*

*aphid*

### Spider Mites

Spider mites are tiny arachnids that are almost invisible to the eye. They suck the sap out of leaves, and the first sign that you have them may be that your leaves begin to "bronze," or take on a brown discoloration. The leaves will eventually die and drop off the plants. Another sign of spider mites is fine webbing between the leaves and stems of your plants. Spider mites are most prevalent in the hot, dry days of summer. To check for spider mites, shake the damaged leaves over a sheet of white paper. Observe carefully, using a magnifying glass if possible. If you see tiny spots that move, there's a good chance you have spider mites. The safest control is to use a strong, fine stream of water to knock them off the plants.

*spider mite*

### Beetles

A number of beetles like to eat plants, but some beetles, such as the ladybug, are good for the garden. Be sure to identify beetles to learn if they are friend or foe. Some beetles, such as cucumber beetles and Japanese beetles, can do a great deal of damage in a short time as they chew on your leaves and flowers. The simplest control is to pick them off by hand.

*Japanese beetles*

### Caterpillars

Caterpillars can have voracious appetites and can cause a great deal of damage to plants. Fortunately, they are easy to spot and can be picked off plants easily. However, don't be too quick to remove caterpillars. While some can do a great amount of damage in a short period of time, you don't want to get rid of a caterpillar that might become a beautiful butterfly.

Reference books on butterflies and moths will help you identify which caterpillar you have. If you decide to capture a caterpillar and bring it inside to observe, be sure to find out what kind it is and what it eats. Some caterpillars are very particular and will die if they don't have the exact food they require.

### Ants

Keep an eye out for ants. Our children became fascinated with the ants in our garden and worked hard at counting anthills and documenting their experiences with ants. While ants don't do any harm to the garden themselves, they are attracted to honeydew, which is a substance excreted by insects such as aphids, mealybugs, whiteflies, and scales. Ants sometimes even carry aphids to healthy plants to keep up the production of honeydew. While we don't advocate trying to rid your garden of ants, if you have ants in your garden, you might check to see if they are an indication of other insects.

### Slugs and Snails

Slugs and snails make fascinating research subjects for indoor study. These slimy creatures (which are related to clams and oysters) can be interesting pets, if kept in an aquarium. They're easy to tell apart, since snails have a hard shell and slugs are soft-bodied. Because they leave a shiny trail wherever they go, children enjoy searching for them in the garden.

Slugs and snails must remain moist at all times, so they usually hide in damp places during the day and come out at night to feed. For this reason, you may not see them eating your plants, but the signs that they have been around are often clear.

You should avoid snail bait, as it is dangerous for young children, and beer, the favorite bait of many gardeners, is probably not appropriate for most early childhood programs. We've included a recipe in this book for a yeast-based bait that you can try. Our children, who were annoyed that slugs were decimating our hostas, became enthusiastic in their quest to drown the slugs in this mixture. (See sidebar in chapter 1.) We can't vouch for its effectiveness, since we didn't catch any slugs, but the experience of making it was worthwhile. Our slug problem was solved once our hostas grew and became healthy enough to withstand some munching.

### Birds

*purple finch*

Okay, we don't really think birds are pests. We love them and want them to come into our garden, and the children have spent many hours observing, drawing, and recording their observations about our birds. However, if the birds are consuming your blueberries or carrying off your sunflower seeds before you have a chance to harvest them, you might find the birds annoying. If you do, discuss the problem with the children and determine together what you want to do. The suggestions detailed at the beginning of this section might prove helpful.

*Mammals*

Depending on where you live, you may have a variety of species of mammals that visit your garden. We have squirrels, rabbits, and chipmunks. You might also experience raccoons and deer. Because we have enjoyed our encounters with these animals, we haven't made any attempt to keep them away from the garden, even though we have been frustrated at times by their intervention.

For example, it took us three years to grow a sunflower house because the squirrels kept stealing the seeds. The chipmunks were blamed for eating all of the ferns we planted in the dinosaur garden, as well as uprooting our morning glory seedlings. (We can't be sure this is what happened, but these were the conclusions the children came to after studying the situation. In fact, slugs may have been at fault for the disappearance of the ferns.) In the case of the sunflower house, we simply kept trying new techniques until one worked—planting three packets of seed and hoping at least some would come up. In other situations we gave up—ferns are expensive, so we decided we would have to do without. You will also want to evaluate any damage mammals do to your garden and determine what, if any, steps you want to take to deal with them.

We do want to caution you in two areas. First, be aware that some mammals carry rabies and other diseases. Whenever we see a sick or strange-acting animal on our playground, we immediately call animal control to come get it. This has only happened a couple of times, over more than a decade, but it is important that children be kept away from sick animals, which are likely to bite if disturbed.

The other concern you may need to deal with is children chasing the animals. Our campus squirrels are accustomed to people and very brave. Because of this, they come close to the children. Children delight in chasing squirrels, so we spend a great deal of energy curbing this behavior. We are aware that it would be possible for a child to corner a squirrel, which might then bite out of fear. Our children are taught that chasing any wild animal is unacceptable.

## Harvesting

Once your garden is established, you can reap the educational benefits of harvesting with young children. Much learning occurs through picking, preparing, and using flowers, produce, and herbs. Again, the teacher plays a vital role in the learning process through modeling and guiding in small groups. Programs with summer sessions will find harvesting to be a perpetual source of joy to the children.

## Picking and Cleaning

The children will likely need help identifying when a particular fruit, vegetable, or herb is ready for harvest. Teachers can facilitate this process by providing a variety of reference books with color photographs of the actual plants in the garden. This way, if children are unsure about the readiness of a particular plant, they can be referred to these resources. Key words such as "green," "unripe," "ripe," "overripe," "rotten," and "spoiled" should be emphasized. Coaching may be needed for harvesting techniques for various plants. Some require clipping, while others lend themselves to snapping, digging, cutting, or pulling. Using these terms with children builds vocabulary and understanding.

We suggest you also incorporate various math skills into harvesting. For instance, when we harvested our green beans, we asked each child to look at the bowl full of beans and to estimate how many were there. Then we counted the actual number of beans, which turned out to be much larger than predicted. Next, we snapped the beans into smaller pieces for cooking. At this point, the children wanted to guess and count again. We did, with some guesses getting much closer the second time. Similarly, the weight of pumpkins can be predicted and measured with a scale, while the length of carrots can be estimated and determined with a ruler. Children can also learn to classify and sort while harvesting. For example, peppers can be sorted into piles of red and green, hot and mild.

Produce should be rinsed thoroughly under running water after harvest and before cooking. We used large colanders at child-size sinks, so children could become fully engaged in this process. Take photographs at all stages of picking and cleaning and record children's comments and reactions in group or individual journals.

## Cooking

Gardening leads to cooking, and cooking leads to wonderful learning opportunities. Children will read recipe charts, measure ingredients, learn about sanitation and safety, observe changes in matter, and experience the nutritional benefits of gardening firsthand. Many parents were shocked to find out that their children ate raw broccoli or red leaf lettuce at school, when they had never done so at home. The key here seems to have been motivation. When children feel invested in something, they are more willing to take risks in order to reap the benefits of their labor. The act of gardening exposed the children to the taste, smell, and texture of many new vegetables and herbs.

Teachers can incorporate literacy skills into cooking by providing various cookbooks and gardening magazines for children to explore. All recipes used for cooking in small groups should be printed onto recipe charts. Recipe charts for younger children can include the use of cutout magazine pictures or drawings to facilitate emergent literacy and the awareness of environmental print. We like to read each step of the recipe aloud as we cook, calling attention to key words and mathematical concepts. We recommend laminating your favorite recipe posters.

Recipe cards can also be used to create a workstation for children to use individually or in pairs during work time. With this technique, one step is written and illustrated on each card, beginning with the most basic

### Entry from Garden Journal, July 1996

We picked green beans in the afternoon. Katie thought we picked nine. Michelle predicted there were 20. Alexia guessed three. Nandy also said there were three beans. We counted the green beans. There were 75 in all.

After we snapped them, we decided to count them again. Michelle guessed there would be 100 pieces of bean. We counted 199 pieces.

July 28, 1997

### Fried Green Tomatoes

Last week the preschoolers found three large green tomatoes on the ground. We decided to try them fried! First we cracked two eggs and poured in some milk. We stirred them together. We dipped the tomato in the mixture and in flour. Then we fried it in vegetable oil. This is what the preschoolers thought:

"They're sour."

"They taste like yucky."

"It's sour." "Do you like it?" "Yes"

"It definitely tastes like a fried green tomato. I haven't had one in years." —Lori (Kati's mom)

"It's good, but I don't know what it is."

"It's not so good" —Louis

"It's good." Thumbs up. —Daniel (Louis' Dad)

## Journal entry from May 6, 1998

We invited our parents to a picnic at CDL. We made Purple Pansy Pumpernickel Sandwiches for appetizers. The following dictation was taken:

"We picked the pansies. Then you get some bread. Then you get some cream cheese. You wash the pansies in water. Then you put the pansies on the sandwiches. Then you eat them." Kasey

"You couldn't really taste the flower. It looked like flowers. Half the bread was white. I ate about three." Neil

"I ate the flower. It didn't taste good, but the cream cheese and the bread taste good." Hodge

"They are called pumpernickel pansies sandwiches. It tastes good. It had all good vitamins in it." Dorsey

"I ate a pansy pumpernickel sandwich. It felt soft and fuzzy in my mouth. You can hardly taste the flower." Marla (teacher)

step of washing your hands and sanitizing the workspace. Each of the required steps is then provided on the following cards, including instructions for cleaning and preparing the workspace for the next student. This strategy works well with older, more independent children.

When creating recipe charts or cards, be sure to use pictures and symbols in the rebus format to aid children in developing reading skills. *Simple Cooking Fun* (Draznin 1997) provides an excellent source for illustrations of common foods, techniques, and cooking utensils. These drawings can be photocopied, cut, colored, and pasted directly onto your rebus chart. In fact, older preschoolers can assist teachers in making these charts. You can laminate charts that will be used repeatedly. Always use actual cooking terminology to provide the most realistic experience and expose children to new vocabulary. For instance, recipes and charts can require them to dice tomatoes, shred cabbage, simmer green beans, or marinate cucumbers.

Children also learn a great deal from preparing one food in a variety of ways. Boil and mash potatoes, as well as baking them whole, french frying, or shredding them for potato pancakes. Roast pumpkin seeds and use the pumpkin to make cookies or pie. Eat cucumbers raw, dice them into a salad, or make them into pickles. Herbs can be dried in open air or in a dehydrator or used fresh. We used some herbs at school, sending the remainder home with children in clear, labeled storage bags for family cooking.

Remember that experimentation is good and that not every recipe will be a huge success. After the children found three large green tomatoes that had fallen from the vine, we decided to make fried green tomatoes, which was a first for all of us. After the activity, we took dictation from the children. They described the fried green tomatoes as "sour," "yucky," and "not so good." The learning experience, however, was wonderful.

We suggest looking for recipes that call for several of the items you have grown in the garden. This reduces your grocery bill and allows the children to see the full potential of the garden. For example, we made salsa, which used tomatoes, red peppers, and green peppers from our garden. We also used these same ingredients to later make mini pizzas on English muffins. Our coleslaw recipe combined carrots and cabbage, while a tossed salad incorporated lettuce, cucumbers, radishes, and tomatoes. Another favorite combination recipe, Basil-Tomato Pie, paired fresh basil with tomatoes. You will find some of our favorite recipes in chapter 8.

Many adults and children in our program were especially surprised by the use of flowers in various recipes. Nasturtiums can be added to salads to make them prettier. Sage flowers can be cut, dipped in batter made from a purchased fritter mix, and fried to make Sage Brochette. We also created masterpieces such as Marigold Cheesecake and Pumpernickel Pansy Sandwiches. These make excellent recipes for garden parties, picnics, and other festive celebrations, such as birthdays and end-of-the-year events.

## Creative Use of Garden Products

In addition to cooking, we found a variety of other ways to utilize items harvested from the garden. We hung gourds to dry indoors. Once dry, we used them to make vases, birdhouses, and maracas. Zinnia, strawflowers, aster, and marigolds were cut and used in both fresh and dry flower arrangements. One day, while cutting flowers, three preschool girls decided to use

**Journal entry from July 9, 1996**

Michelle and Kati cut flowers outside. They decided the flowers would be great for a wedding. Michelle was the bride.
   "I was the bride and Jo was the priest." Kati was the sister who held Michelle's dress.

the flowers to act out a wedding ceremony. Using dried flowers from our garden, we made sweet-smelling potpourri sachets to give as gifts. Hollyhock dolls, created on the playground, sparked creative dramatic-play scenarios. We suggest you subscribe to garden magazines or ask parents to donate old ones. They are full of creative recipes, ideas, and projects.

## Harvesting and Saving Seeds

When you think about harvesting, don't forget to glean seeds from your garden to plant next year. Children can learn a great deal from identifying, collecting, and saving their own seeds. The seeds of annual plants lend themselves to this process since they fulfill their life cycle in one year. Seeds from biennials and perennials can be salvaged as well. However, seeds from hybrid plants (many vegetables, for example) will not usually grow true to form (National Gardening Association 2000). This is one good reason to grow heirloom varieties of many vegetables.

   Encourage children to take seeds from only healthy, thriving plants and to remove all pulp or fiber from the surface of each seed. The best time to harvest each type of seed will vary from plant to plant. Generally, seeds should be allowed to dry naturally on the plant as long as possible. We suggest you try harvesting seeds from vegetables such as beans, peas, peppers, pumpkins, and tomatoes. You might also collect seeds from annual flowers such as zinnias, sunflowers, marigolds, and cosmos. We encourage you to be creative and experimental in this process. You might take seeds from plants you know are hybrids, for example, to allow the children to see whether or not they breed true.

   With help from parents or other volunteers, your class might harvest and sell seeds as a fund-raising project. We read about a class of third and fourth graders in Vermont who worked with their classroom teacher to harvest seeds and enlisted the supervision of their art teacher in

creating marketable seed packets (NGA 2000). These students counted seeds, labeled packets with planting instructions, and sold seeds to community members. This clearly provided a valuable lesson in science, math, economics, and communication.

## Drawing the Project to a Close

At some point, all great garden projects must come to an end. At the end of the project, provide the children with a sense of closure and a chance to reflect on their newly developed competencies (Katz and Chard 1999). This involves the third step of the K-W-L process; summarizing and documenting what children have *Learned*.

Every teacher or group of teachers must analyze the group's current level of interest, measure the desire to move on to a new topic, and decide when to begin the culmination process. The timing can sometimes be tricky, since the learning won't ever be truly finished and won't stop when the project ends. We often look for regular breaks in the school calendar and plan culminating events around them. This helps us avoid starting a new project that will be interrupted by a school vacation. Sometimes, however, a project may be cut short due to lack of interest on the part of the children. It is better to stop a project early than to drag it out until children are bored and turned off to future study of the topic.

At this point, the teacher will want to assist children in identifying unanswered questions and planning for the next gardening experience. This can be done individually or in small groups. This information will be helpful to the teacher if she embarks on a similar project in the future with a new group of children. This information might also allow parents and future teachers to build on the child's current level of knowledge and desire to investigate the topic further.

Sometimes a new project will spin off garden-related issues, or the class might decide to go in a totally new direction based on community resources, current events, or seasonal changes. The teacher's role here is to help the children make a smooth transition to the next project and to build on the new skills they developed through gardening.

## Final Representations: A Last Look at Learning

Throughout the life of the garden, children will use various means to represent what they have learned. When closing a project, children will need assistance in finalizing these representations as they apply and articulate the new concepts they have learned. Teachers can facilitate the final representation of new knowledge by helping children to review garden journals and select their best work. At this point, some children might even want to consolidate their learning by adding dictation to sketches or redrawing them completely to fill in previously missed details. Others will want to write a few final pages in their journal to summarize their thoughts and feelings about the overall gardening process. Children will be motivated to engage in these tasks if they are working toward meaningful goals, such as a planning a culminating event or creating a classroom display.

## Culminating Events

Culminating events are a great way to bring closure to a project by providing opportunities to exhibit the work of the project to an audience. The active planning of culminating events provides children with the motivation to consolidate and apply newly acquired information. This can be done in a variety of ways, depending on the children's developmental level and individual interests. The teacher needs to guide the children in making decisions about the type of event to plan. The younger the children, the more you will need to lead. For instance, you can suggest an event to younger children and then invite their full participation in the preparations. On the other hand, you might interview kindergarten students about their ideas for ways to present and communicate their learning to others.

Parties, open houses, and a visit from another class are examples of excellent culminating events. Regardless of the type of event selected, you will need to think about the audience. Would your children feel comfortable presenting their learning to parents and community members, or would they rather invite another class from your school? Would they like to do an

oral presentation with a slide show, perform through drama and song, or provide tours of the garden and other classroom displays? These are decisions that each teacher must make based on the confidence and skill levels of her students.

Our favorite culminating event was a garden party for families, contributing community members, and other classes at our preschool. The teachers suggested this event to the children and then solicited their ideas and involvement. One of our major concerns in planning this event was to ensure that the children felt ownership of the party and the process. We wanted the party to be full of their ideas and to clearly represent their learning. We started by asking the children how to plan a party. Many of the children knew that invitations were necessary, while others suggested food and games. Some children mentioned wearing party clothes and listening to music at parties they had attended.

Based on the children's prior knowledge of parties, we embarked on the process of planning our culminating event. First, we invited the children to draw garden-related pictures for the invitations on business-card-size slips of paper. This allowed for several children's artwork to be used in the final copy. Another way we ensured child ownership was to allow the children to select their favorite recipes, based on the cooking experiences we had previously provided and the current available herbs, flowers, and vegetables in the garden. Our final menu was indeed festive, including Marigold Cheesecake, Basil-Tomato Pies, Chive Potato Pancakes, and Pumpernickel Pansy Sandwiches.

With the party fast approaching, the children prepared to provide guided tours of their favorite sections of the garden to party-goers. One way that we prepared them for this was to hold a garden scavenger hunt, as described in chapter 7. The children were given small cards with the picture and name of a certain plant. In this way, they learned to locate and name the herbs, flowers, and vegetables very quickly. On party day, many guests and parents were impressed by the preschoolers' ability to discriminate between plants such as basil and sage.

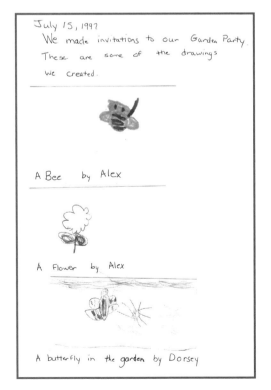

July 15, 1997

We made invitations to our Garden Party. These are some of the drawings we created.

A Bee by Alex

A Flower by Alex

A butterfly in the garden by Dorsey

To incorporate music, the children selected a favorite song, from our new repertoire of songs and poems about gardening, to perform at the party. A note was sent home to parents asking for volunteers to play live music in the garden during the event. One parent played the flute, while others agreed to play their guitars. Other festivities included the making of party hats from newspaper, glue, sequins, and feathers, as well as bubble blowing from the sensory table. The teachers created a program to be used on party day that explained the various sections of the garden and included quotations from the children about each.

For a week before the event, the children harvested produce and prepared food for the party. They weeded the garden, filled bird feeders and birdbaths, and picked up litter from the playground. We also prepared a guest book where visitors could sign in and provide feedback. All of these activities helped children consider social skills and experience a sense of community while working toward the shared goal of hosting a party.

## Displays

Displays provide another avenue for children to reflect on and communicate to others what they have learned. Teachers can encourage children to review all relevant sketches and journals and then form small groups to create murals with clearly labeled details. Some children might choose to represent the various plants in the garden. One way to do this is to transfer the

color from each plant onto a large white sheet by pounding it with a rock (see "Crushed Kaleidoscope" activity in chapter 7). Other groups might want to make a mural about the tools and techniques used while mulching, watering, weeding, and deadheading. Yet another group may want to create a mural of a fieldwork site, such as a water garden or flower shop, based on photos, videos, and sketches from the trip.

Photographs taken over the life of the project also lend themselves to beautiful and meaningful displays. In preparation for our garden party, we created four large posters with the following headings—"Before and After," "Planting," "Tending," and "Harvesting." Photographs were mounted on each poster and then various children were asked to tell what they were doing in each picture. The children's statements were then typed on a computer and printed for mounting on the posters. This was another way for the preschoolers to share what they had been learning with their parents, peers, and visitors.

Displays can be three-dimensional, such as a collection of garden tools, seed packets, soil types, vegetables, reference books, and measurement instruments, such as a rain gauge and thermometer. Try preparing one tray full of garden products to stimulate each of the five senses (see "You Fill Up My Senses" in chapter 7). Other displays might involve a collection of matted artwork and handwritten stories created at various stages of the project. Charts and graphs could be included with children's written anecdotal accounts of the scientific processes used. Finally, don't forget to display your concept web showing the topics covered and the original charts from the first two steps in K-W-L, so that parents and children can compare beginning knowledge with project outcomes.

## References

Barash, Cathy Wilkinson. 1995. *Edible flowers: From garden to palate.* Golden, Colo.: Fulcrum Publishing.

Draznin, Sharon. 1997. *Simple cooking fun.* Huntington Beach, Calif.: Teacher Created Materials.

Katz, Lilian, and Sylvia Chard. 1999. *The project approach.* Norwood, N.J.: Ablex Publishing Corporation.

National Gardening Association (NGA). 2000. Seed-saving stewards. *Growing Ideas: A Journal of Garden-based Learning,* 11 (2): pages 1, 16.

Starcher, Allison Mia. 1998. *Good bugs for your garden.* Chapel Hill, N.C.: Algonquin Books of Chapel Hill.

# 6

# Frequently Asked Questions

**What is happening in the rest of the classroom while the garden project is going on?**

As with any project, the garden experience will spill over into most areas of the classroom and curriculum. Many learning centers lend themselves to garden-related activities. We incorporated these activities into our housekeeping area, math and fine-motor area, reading corner, writing table, art area, and sensory table.

The housekeeping area, for instance, allows children to apply the new concepts they have acquired and engage in spontaneous peer teaching around the topic. Make-believe experiences allow children to explore some of the cultural, social, and economic reasons for gardening. For instance, our children interacted with a flower-shop prop box for several consecutive days following a fieldwork trip. They used plastic vases, silk flowers, tissue paper, florist foam, small pots, receipt pads, play money, cash registers, telephones, and gift cards to reenact what they had seen on the trip. This occurred both in the housekeeping area and in a sensory table full of potting soil. This type of play was repeated and refined over a period of weeks, with teachers adding new ideas, such as using a credit card as payment or sending flowers to a funeral, when interest waned.

The children also engaged in dramatic endeavors related to cooking with products from the garden. As they gained experience with harvesting, cleaning, and preparing various unfamiliar herbs and flowers in diverse ways, they often carried these themes to the sandbox or house corner. This type of play sometimes occurred in the garden as well, since our trellis house provided the perfect spot for

pretending to cook and eat vegetables. Our cooking prop box facilitated this type of play by providing motivating and stimulating props, such as colanders for rinsing flowers and herbs, small cutting boards with play knives, and vegetable scrub brushes.

Garden-related activities can also be implemented in the math and fine-motor area of the classroom. Children can sort and classify various seeds, leaves, and vegetables. Plastic fruits and vegetables can be sorted in several different ways. You can create homemade math games, such as the "Garden Leaf Memory Game" and the "Seed to Plant Matchup" described in chapter 7. Children can apply math skills by using rulers, scales, and tape measures to measure the length, weight, and circumference of various vegetables. Charts and graphs about garden data can be created and posted in this area. In addition, a variety of puzzles and displays showing plant parts, insects, and garden creatures can be purchased commercially for classroom use.

Your reading corner can be stocked with children's literature about gardening, as well as many high-quality reference books on the subject (see appendix 1, "Children's Books about Gardens and Garden Creatures"). In this area, you will also want to include samples of the children's writing about the garden. If research teams have created books to represent their learning on fieldwork trips, place them on the shelf for others to read. You might also create handmade class books, such as a garden alphabet book (see "A-B-C You in the Garden" in chapter 7).

The writing center provides children with opportunities to apply emergent literacy skills to meaningful projects. The garden journal, or blank pages of the journal, can be placed in this area to encourage children to record their daily gardening chores and discoveries, as well as

7·7·00

Sara brought a story about how plants grow. We talked about what grows above ground and what grows below ground.

I was putting them on the board. I was putting on — I don't know.

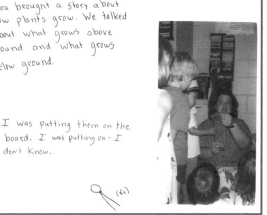

new questions that need answering. After cooking with produce from the garden, children can proceed to the writing center to recall and record the recipe on a poster using invented spelling or give dictation to the teacher about the cooking experience. The poster could then be displayed for parents and visitors to review. Eventually, you could create a class cookbook by compiling the children's representations of their favorite recipes. The writing table also provides teachers with the opportunity to take dictation about the garden for the class or school newsletter. Toward the end of the project, children can work in this area to create a guest list, menu, invitations, programs, and a guest book for a culminating event or party.

As children become fascinated with the array of colors and creatures in the garden, they will begin to spontaneously represent their learning using various media in the art area. Teachers can facilitate this process by providing a variety of materials and allowing children time and space to create. If children need inspiration, adults can try the following ideas:

✸ Place a vase full of fresh cut flowers or a bowl full of vegetables from the garden on the art table with paper and oil pastels.

✸ Place the art easel by a window with a view of the garden, or put it outside in the garden with various colors of paint.

✸ Select and pick leaves from plants. Place the leaves on the art table with paper and peeled crayons. Show children how to cover each leaf with paper and rub with the side of the crayon to create leaf rubbings.

✸ Provide a wide variety of seeds, as well as glue and child-size shoebox lids, for making seed mosaics. Use photographs, posters, or art books to introduce the children to mosaics (arranging and mounting many tiny items to create a larger picture).

✸ Allow children to roll out a flat surface on clay and then make prints of various leaves, roots, and vegetables (such as carrot, cucumber, and green bean). Encourage children to carve the name of each plant into the clay using a pencil or toothpick. These plant impressions can be allowed to dry and used later as a class display.

✸ Use an overhead projector to project a simple drawing of your garden design onto the wall. Place butcher paper over the projected garden design and trace it using a dark felt-tip marker. Remove the overhead projector and allow children to color and label the garden design with markers.

Finally, many aspects of gardening can be explored at the sensory table. Here, children will engage the senses as they feel, smell, and observe various plants and materials. Clean wood chips, often used for mulch, can be scooped, poured, and measured rather than sand, as long as the chips are free of chemicals. Various planting materials and soils can be explored, as described in the "Soiled Again!" learning experience in chapter 7. Herbs, such as mint or basil, can be picked and placed in water to investigate their varied aromas (see "What's That Smell?" in chapter 7). Finally, bean seeds can be planted and sprouted in the potting soil to provide children with an up close look at the germination process (see "Little Sprouts" in chapter 7).

## How do I work the garden project into the daily routine?

You can work in garden activities throughout the day to provide the children with a well-rounded curriculum. Here are some ideas for different times of the day.

## Group Meeting or Circle Time

⊛ Introduce new materials, plants, and objects of interest that you will be using in the garden. Pass them around and discuss how they will be used.

⊛ Introduce new books about gardens and garden-related topics.

⊛ Invite a guest to share information about gardening. (Make sure the guest brings artifacts and is able to interest children in a lively manner.)

⊛ Share the garden journal or other representations with each other.

⊛ Do creative dramatics. For instance, have the children pretend to be seeds. As the seeds are watered and as the sun shines, the seeds grow into tall, healthy plants stretching for the sun.

⊛ Act out different parts of gardening: weeding, hoeing, mulching, and so forth.

## Story Time

⊛ Read fictional books about gardens, such as *The Carrot Seed* by Ruth Kraus.

⊛ Examine reference books and look for children's interests. These observations will help you later in your planning.

⊛ Work on reading and writing in garden journal.

⊛ Tell traditional garden stories, such as the story about the turnip that wouldn't come up. You may want to produce flannelboard or magnetboard pieces for these stories.

⊛ Make up stories about the garden, including the names of the children in your group. Allow the children to contribute to the story as you go along.

## Music Time

⊛ Sing and play songs with a garden theme, such as David Mallett's "Garden Song." (Available on Peter, Paul, and Mary's album, *Peter, Paul, and Mommy Too*, from Warner Brothers Records, Inc., Burbank, Calif. 1993.)

⊛ Make up songs or adapt songs you know to a garden theme, involving the children in the process. For instance, "Down by the Bay" can become "Down by the Garden" with the children making up silly verses. "Five Little Pumpkins Sitting on a Gate" can become "Five Little Ladybugs Sitting on a Leaf."

⊛ Have the children move to music as though they are plants in the garden.

## What if some of the children aren't interested in gardening?

Regardless of the project you choose, children's levels of involvement will vary. Gardening is no exception to this rule. This should not cause concern as long as the majority of your class shows interest in creating and exploring the garden. Some children will be very motivated to begin the project, while others will have their curiosity aroused as the garden comes to life before their eyes. Some will be most excited about the actual digging, watering, and mulching, while others are fascinated with cooking or representing the garden through art and literacy activities. The garden project is not intended to be the sole source of learning in your classroom. Rather, it should complement and enhance the existing curriculum. High-quality classrooms will have basic experiences at their core, such as several kinds of blocks; sensory tables; areas for art, literacy, science, and math; manipulatives, games, and puzzles; dramatic play; music; and possibly computers.

Finally, we want to caution you against starting more than one project at a time, which makes it difficult to support the full, in-depth investigation of each topic. Rather than researching two or more topics simultaneously, we recommend that you observe and document the interests of the uninvolved children and use this information to plan for your next learning theme or project.

Teachers who face half-day schedules, or those who have different children on Monday, Wednesday, and Friday than on Tuesday and Thursday, should still focus on one broad project, such as gardening. Then with each class of children, decide on the group focus. For instance, the morning class might be most interested in growing, cutting, arranging, and preserving flowers, while the afternoon group might focus on cooking with herbs and vegetables. For more detailed information on how to guide projects while managing split schedules refer to *Young Investigators: The Project Approach in the Early Years* (Helm and Katz 2001).

# What adjustments should I make if my children are younger or older than the children at CDL?

Our primary experience in gardening with young children has been with children ages three to six. Our children move to the preschool when they are three years old and stay until they enter kindergarten. Some return for the summer after they finish kindergarten. The experiences we

share in this book are essentially for children in this age range. However, we have also had some experience including our infants and toddlers in garden activities, and we know of many primary school programs that involve children in gardening. If you are working with infants, toddlers, or school-age children, you may choose to adapt this book to work for your children. Here are some guidelines to keep in mind as you do so.

## Gardening with Infants and Toddlers

While infants and toddlers will not be able to understand the garden at the same level older children do, they certainly show curiosity and appreciation for plants and flowers. In fact, you only need to watch a group of toddlers in a field of dandelions to see how captivated they are by the fluffy yellow blooms and the fragile puffs. It is easy for teachers to build on this innate interest by introducing these youngest children to cultivated plantings.

You do need to take a number of precautions when sharing plants with infants and toddlers. Anyone who works with children this age understands their inclination to put objects in their mouths. Obviously, plants that have any toxic components, no matter how mild, should be avoided. Also, plants that produce berries, which could be choked on, should be excluded.

Naturally, very young children test new objects by pulling and prodding. Because of this, delicate plants have no place in the infant-toddler garden. If the children are left to their own devices, you may find that the produce is pulled from the vine long before it is ready .

To meet the special needs of our children under three years of age, we have taken the following steps:

    ※ We set aside a section of the preschool garden for use by the toddlers. They plant this area and tend it, under the watchful eye of their teachers. Because this area is not within their play area, they are always closely supervised when they are in contact with the plants. They visit the space a couple times a week. Of course, sometimes they pull up the plants, but this happens occasionally with the older children as well.

    ※ We take the infants and toddlers for frequent visits to the preschool garden, as well as other nearby gardens. They are enthralled by the colors and scents of the plants and occasionally pick flowers to take back with them.

    ※ We include plants on the toddler playground that are hardy and unlikely to be destroyed by curious fingers. The most successful of these have been herbs, such as basil, mints, and sage. Marigolds and zinnias work well too. We put these plants in large pots or boxes and allow them to grow strong roots before introducing them to the toddlers. Once the plants are firmly rooted, it is unlikely that the children will be able to pull them out of the soil. Because these plants actually benefit from deadheading, it doesn't usually harm them if the children pull the flowers off. And the herbs have the added benefit of providing a wonderful scent. We have even noticed young infants who are not yet walking sniffing the plants.

## Gardening with Primary-age Children

Because a garden project incorporates all aspects of the curriculum, it is an excellent topic for school-age children to explore. Many elementary teachers are discovering the benefits of involving children in gardening, and an increasing number of schools are now incorporating gardens into their curriculum. A search of "school gardens" on the Internet results in many stories from classrooms and schools that are introducing children to growing plants.

Much of the information in this book can also be used in designing and building gardens for primary schools. The guidelines for garden design and installation are the same regardless of the purpose of the garden. In addition, the information on the project approach is also applicable to schoolagers, and many teachers successfully incorporate projects in their elementary classes. Some of the activities included in this book can be used as they are written, but others will need to be adapted to challenge older children.

Some further suggestions for working with primary-age children include the following:

Team up with other classrooms to create a school garden. This way, each class can plant and maintain a specific section of the garden, while sharing responsibilities for common duties, such as watering over weekends and school breaks.

Pair older students with kindergarten or preschool children as "garden buddies." This will facilitate journaling, encourage cooperative learning, and build a sense of community within the school.

Involve the children in the planning stages of the garden. One story of how this can be done is in *Bringing Reggio Emilia Home: An Innovative Approach to Early Childhood Education* (Cadwell 1997).

Have children keep individual journals documenting their experiences.

Take advantage of the longer attention spans of these children by involving them in experiments that take several weeks to complete. Have them carefully record changes that occur during the course of these experiments.

Allow the children to use a camera to record changes as they occur. This will help them in making comparisons over a period of time.

Work to keep children challenged. By observing the children's interest and growing knowledge, the teacher can design learning experiences that will keep them moving toward gaining new information.

We believe that this book is a good starting point for primary teachers. In fact, some of the pictures in this book are of our graduates who returned to visit the garden. We have found that they still remember much of what they learned of gardening when they were with us and that their interest is as keen as ever. We trust that this will be the experience of many elementary-school children. Every gardener, regardless of age or experience, knows that there is always something new to discover in the garden. In fact, the power of a classroom garden is that no matter how long you garden, you will always have something left to learn.

# What do we do if our school doesn't operate during the summer?

In planning for your garden, you will need to think about your school calendar. If you operate year-round, your only limits in selecting what to plant are determined by your climate. However, if you operate on a nine-month calendar, or are closed at odd times, you'll have to take this into consideration when determining what and how you will plant. We are on an academic calendar with two semesters and an eight-week summer session. Although we are open during academic breaks, only a few children come during those times and much of our key staff is off. Therefore, it is important that our garden is fully planted by the second week in May and that we make arrangements for someone to water regularly over the four-week break, or we will come back to a dried-up garden.

If you are on a nine-month calendar and are closed during the summer, you are missing out on a large part of the growing season, especially if you are in a colder climate. Here are some ideas for teachers who are struggling with this dilemma:

| Cool Weather Crops | |
|---|---|
| spinach | cauliflower |
| lettuce | cabbage |
| broccoli | kale |
| peas | beets |
| carrots | collards |
| radishes | |

✳ As soon as school begins, plant cool weather crops and plants that will grow quickly before winter comes.

✳ Plant bulbs. Many bulbs need to be planted in the fall and then produce a colorful show just when you need relief from the long winter. Just a few examples are jonquils, tulips, hyacinths, daffodils, crocuses, and irises. In addition, many bulbs can be forced by placing the bulbs in the refrigerator, then bringing them into the classroom where it is warm. You can find information on how to do this in any bulb book or you can buy paperwhite narcissus and amaryllis bulbs ready to force. This is a great project to keep children interested as they wait for the ground to thaw and the bulbs to poke out of the ground outdoors. We suggest you plant a variety of bulbs, paying attention to when they will bloom. This way you can have a continuous show from the early crocuses, which will come up even through snow, to the bulbs that emerge in late spring, such as late tulips and irises.

✳ Plant an indoor garden by making use of sunny windows and plant lights.

✳ Work cooperatively with another program that is open year-round. Many child care centers would be thrilled to have someone help them get seeds started over the winter so they could have plants to tend to in the summer. After the plants are ready to plant, the children from both schools can work to put them in the ground, and your children can help tend them until the end of the school year. When school starts again in the fall, you can visit the garden and find out how it did over the summer.

✳ Plant a garden and plan to meet at a set time each week over the summer to water, weed, and harvest. This will take a lot of dedication on your part, and not all of your students will become involved, but for children and parents who do, it will be a rewarding experience. Children who participate can keep a journal of their activities to share at the beginning of the school year.

✳ Build a greenhouse. While this may not be feasible for every school, if you can find a way to do it you will have numerous opportunities for winter garden activities. Remember that there are many kinds of greenhouses and not all are exorbitantly expensive. You may have a parent with the skill to design and build a greenhouse, and you may have parents or community members who are willing to donate materials.

⊛ Use cold frames. You can start plants early by using cold frames. These are simple, wooden boxes with glass or thick Plexiglas tops that can be opened to let the air out if it gets too hot. With a cold frame, you extend the length of your garden season. Cold frames can be built easily or purchased ready to go.

Whatever you elect to do, don't avoid gardening because you have a difficult school schedule. The rewards of gardening are well worth some thought and adaptation on your part.

## What can we do in the winter when there is no garden?

If you live in a climate where the winters are cold, a lot of your curriculum during that time will be unrelated to gardening. This break will be a good time for you to think ahead and plan for the next year. Of course, children can participate in garden-related activities during this time, for instance by caring for plants in the classroom, exploring garden materials, or caring for garden creatures. Worm composting is a year-round job and children never seem to tire of caring for and exploring worms.

As the end of winter nears, the teacher can introduce garden catalogs and start planning the new garden season with the children. Seeds can be started as spring draws near so that plants are ready for the garden when the frost-free date arrives.

## How will the garden be different after the first year?

During the first year, much of your time and energy will go into designing and building your garden. At this time, input from adults is essential. But once the basic garden is in you will find you are free to explore and experiment with the children, becoming even more responsive to their suggestions.

In subsequent years, involve the children in selecting any annuals that need to be replaced in the garden as well as including some new perennials. If you have some of the same children, go back to the final documentation of the original project. You should have written notes or dictation about questions that still needed answering. Share this information with the children, encouraging them to think about what they learned last year and which of the remaining questions they would like to explore. Engage the children in discussions about their favorite garden activities and how they could extend them this year.

In the years to follow, work with the children to come up with new topics to study. We found that after the first year, our

7-11-00

We planted bug-eating plants in the terrarium.

Bug eating plants. They chomp down on bugs. (Alexis)

I'm looking at some flowers that eat some bugs.

focus moved from general (gardening) to specific (flowers, herbs, garden structures). Look for opportunities to investigate such topics in-depth.

## How do I prevent damage to the garden from outsiders?

One concern of many teachers may be the threat of vandalism in the garden. In some areas, teachers may be worried enough that they will want to limit the access to the garden with a fence or other barrier. We were a bit anxious when we first built our garden, because a large part of it lies outside our fence along a fairly busy sidewalk. We were especially concerned that, if the college students got a bit rambunctious, our garden would be in their path. We wanted to protect the work of our children.

One of the first steps we took was making a sign for the garden, which we posted in a prominent place. It said, "This garden is planted and cared for by the children of the Child Development Laboratories. Please be gentle." This did the trick. Although people pass our garden throughout the day, we've never had a problem with vandals. In fact, we've hardly ever had anyone take vegetables from the garden, even though it's just a few steps from the sidewalk.

If you are very concerned about vandalism, in addition to signs, you might also want to alert neighbors to help you by keeping an eye on the garden when you're not around. Also consider involving community members in the garden. The more people who feel ownership, the less likely harm will be done. Our experience has been that people often respect the work more when they know children are invested in it. The more you can spread this message, the more likely you will be to avoid problems.

*house finch*

# References

Cadwell, Louise Boyd. 1997. *Bringing Reggio Emilia home: An innovative approach to early childhood education.* New York: Teachers College Press.

Helm, Judy Harris, and Lilian Katz. 2001. *Young investigators: The project approach in the early years.* New York: Teachers College Press.

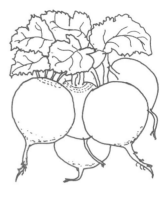

# 7

# Universal Garden Learning Experiences

*P*eople often comment that children in their early years have short attention spans. We take exception to this theory. Children have short attention spans when adults direct their learning and determine for them how they should spend their time. However, when children are allowed to participate in decision making about what they will do, often they will spend immense amounts of time on projects. Any teacher who has worked with children in a classroom that allows for child choice can attest to this.

As you make your way through a garden project, you will be amazed at the interest some children have in the earth and the plants and animals that inhabit it. You will find that many activities are child-initiated or rise naturally from your experiences in the garden. With a little ingenuity, your garden project will be uniquely yours and full of surprises.

When we began our garden, we were frustrated by consulting books on gardening with children. Many of the books consisted of ideas for growing many plants and maybe one activity that could be done with each plant. Since we didn't want to grow a new plant every day, and since plants take time to grow, these books didn't fit our needs. Therefore, our goal in this chapter is to suggest experiences that are not dependent on what plants are being grown, but that can be done in any garden. We hope the following experiences meet that criterion as you seek new adventures in your garden.

# Exploring Plants

## Drink It Up

### Concepts

- Plants need water to live.
- Flowers take up water through their stems.
- Flowers have veins throughout their stems, leaves, and petals.

### Materials

flowers (For best effect, experiment with a variety of flowers. The best for deep color are those with many tiny petals, such as Queen Anne's lace or bridal wreath spirea, but the experiment will work with most white flowers. One of the most dramatic flowers for observing veins in the petals is lily of the valley. However, if you choose to use this flower, close teacher supervision is necessary at all times, since it is poisonous.)

clear vases or other containers (liter soda bottles with the tops cut off work well and won't break)

water

food coloring

knife or scissors for cutting stems

### Description

1. Fill the vase or other container with water. Add a few drops of food coloring to the water.
2. Make a fresh cut on the stems of the flowers. If the stems are soft, you can cut them with scissors, but if they are woody, make a diagonal cut with a knife for best results.
3. Place the flowers in the colored water and observe. Within a few hours, you should start to see the color from the water in the petals of the flowers.
4. With the children, study the petals carefully. A magnifying glass will help in seeing the individual veins of the petals.

### Extensions

- Before placing the flowers in the water, leave some of them out of water for a while. Don't cut the stems of these immediately before placing the flowers in the colored water. Use two separate vases so you can compare the absorption rates of flowers with freshly cut stems and those that have been left out of the water.
- Use several varieties of flowers and compare the results.

### Safety Considerations

Only the teacher should use a sharp knife. Children may be able to cut with table knives if the stems are not too hard.

# Little Sprouts

## Concepts

- Plants grow from seeds.
- Seeds need moisture to grow.
- Seeds grow roots as well as leaves and stems.

## Materials

sensory table or large tub
potting soil
bean seeds
water
trowels and cultivators

## Description

1. Guide the children in filling the sensory table or tub at least half-full with potting soil.
2. Have the children add water until the soil is moist throughout. This may take a lot of water if the mix is very dry, but be careful not to saturate it to the point where water is standing on the bottom.
3. Add the bean seeds to the tub. The bigger seeds you use, the easier it will be for the children to observe the changes that occur.
4. Let the children use the trowels and cultivators to manipulate the soil and to bury and dig up the beans. Leave the soil and seeds in the tub. Do not cover. Check the beans every day and allow the children to continue to dig in the soil.
5. Notice changes in the seeds as the days pass. They will swell and start to sprout. Roots will form. Let the children handle the seeds and guide them in observing changes.
6. Avoid removing the seeds before the children have had plenty of opportunities to observe the plant growth, but after the seeds are fully sprouted, you may want to transplant the seeds to a planter or to the garden. Have the children carefully tuck the seedlings, roots down, into the soil.

## Extensions

- Have the children draw pictures of the seeds at various stages of development.
- Take dictation as children describe the changes they see in the seeds.
- Photograph the seeds every couple of days and display the photos of the seeds at various stages.
- Try the above with different seeds, some small and some large. Compare the different varieties of seeds.

## Safety Considerations

Avoid using potting soil with fertilizer or other additives. Use trowels and cultivators with curved, rather than sharp, edges. Be sure children are adequately supervised when using hand tools.

# Texture Walk

## Concepts

⊛ Plants can be identified through the sense of touch.

⊛ Plants can feel smooth, fuzzy, prickly, soft, hard, slick, or bumpy.

⊛ Plants have parts, such as stems, leaves, stalks, vines, petals, fruits, and vegetables.

## Materials

note cards
marker
chart paper or clipboard with paper
a garden in full bloom

## Description

1. Prepare for this activity by writing one texture word on each note card: fuzzy, smooth, prickly, soft, hard, slick, and bumpy.
2. Invite six or seven children to come to the garden with you for a texture walk. Once in the garden, ask children to tell you how plants feel. Accept and acknowledge all answers. Explain that they will be going on a texture walk to find plants that feel a certain way. Show the children the cards one at a time and have them try to read the word. Ask the children if they can think of any things that feel smooth. Repeat this process with each card.
3. Tell the children that each will be given a card with a texture word on it. Then each will go into the garden and try to find a plant that feels the same as the word on the card. Emphasize to children that they must be gentle when touching plants so as not to hurt or kill the plants. Explain that it is not a race, so they will be walking slowly and carefully looking for a plant that might match their card.
4. Remind the children that plants have many parts. Ask the children to name some parts of a plant. Print the parts they list on the chart paper or clipboard. Call attention to any plant parts they might have forgotten. Tell them to check the different plant parts to find out how they feel (for example, the vine might be prickly, but the vegetable might be smooth).Give one card to each child. Make sure each child understands the meaning of the word on their card. Release the children into the garden one at a time, to minimize their urge to race.
5. Follow the children into the garden to provide support as they locate each texture. See if they can name the part of the plant they are feeling.
6. Encourage the children to trade cards and locate new textures until each child has had all the cards.

## Extensions

⊛ After going on several texture walks, children will be ready for this extension. Gather children together near the edge of the garden. Blindfold one child at a time with a handkerchief. Lead the child to a prickly plant (such as cucumber) and place her hands on it. Ask the child to guess the name of the prickly plant. Repeat with another child and another plant (such as fuzzy lamb's ear or a bumpy pumpkin). Continue until all children have had a turn.

⊛ Peel several large crayons. Take clipboards, white paper, and peeled crayons to the garden. Invite the children to make a texture rubbing. Place the plant part between the paper and clipboard (as with a hosta or fern leaf) or place the paper directly on top of the plant (as with a pumpkin). Unless the plant is ready for harvest or grows abundantly in your garden, supervise to be sure that the plant remains intact throughout this process.

# What's That Smell?

## Concepts
- Plants have leaves and roots.
- Many herbs have a distinct smell.
- Herbs are used in many foods we eat.

## Materials
sensory/water table
water
water smocks/aprons
an herb with a strong scent (such as chives, mint, basil, or bee balm)
plastic dishes and utensils
laminated recipe cards or recipe charts that call for the selected herb

## Description
Preparation—Before the children arrive, go to the garden and pick several stalks of a plentiful herb, such as mint. (If you have a lot, pull it up by the roots, so children will be able to examine the whole plant. If you do this, wash off the roots.) Fill the sensory table halfway with water. Place the freshly picked herbs in the water with the pretend cookware and utensils.

1. Invite children to come to the sensory table to look. Allow them time to play in this area and explore the water and herbs.
2. Approach the children, after they have been playing a while, to ask about what they are doing. You might even ask them if they smell something. Discuss the herbs in the table and the kinds of foods that include them (for example, for mint you might discuss candy, tea, ice cream, gum, and so on).
3. Offer the recipe cards and charts to the children and ask if they want to pretend to cook something with the herbs. Read and discuss the recipes with the children and then post them near the sensory table for children to refer to in their dramatic play.

## Extensions
- Use fresh herbs to prepare some of the recipes from the cards or charts.
- Prepare a "Smell the Same" game using fragrant flowers and herbs. Collect empty black film canisters and poke a few small holes in the lid of each. Go to the garden and collect two samples of each fragrant flower or herb (such as rose petals or sage leaves). Place these inside the film canisters. Write the name of the flower or herb on the underside of each cap with a permanent marker and replace it. Ask the children to smell each canister until they find two that smell the same. To check their conclusions, show them how to open the canisters and check to see if the plant names match.

## Garden Leaf Memory Game

### Concepts

- ✳ Plants have leaves.
- ✳ Each plant has leaves of a specific shape, size, and color.
- ✳ Plants can be identified by studying their leaves.

### Materials

blank note cards
marker
Con-Tact paper
pairs of leaves from garden plants

### Description

1. Find at least ten pairs of matching leaves from the garden. The older your children are, the more pairs you will need to make this game challenging. The younger the children, the more distinct the leaves will need to be (parsley versus pumpkin leaf versus basil). You may want to take leaves from your most abundant plants, but you can use a set of clippers to take small cuttings from other plants with unique leaves.
2. Use Con-Tact paper to adhere one leaf to each note card.
3. Gather the children together in a small group on the floor or at a table to play a memory game. Mix the cards thoroughly and place them upside down in even rows.
4. Decide which child will start. Have each child turn over two cards. Help the children read the names on the cards and notice the details of the leaves. If the cards match, the child keeps the pair and takes another turn. If they do not match, encourage the children to try to remember what they are and then place them face down. Moving clockwise around the table, the next child takes a turn.
5. When all matches are made, the cards are shuffled and the game begins again. (We prefer to avoid using the term "win" to refer to the child with the most cards. Instead we focus on finishing and starting again.)

### Extensions

- ✳ When this game becomes too easy, ask the children to go into the garden with you to find new pairs of leaves to add to the game. Allow them to assist you in attaching the leaves and printing the plant names on the new cards.
- ✳ Repeat this process with pictures of flowers from seed catalogs, seed packets, or with actual flower petals.
- ✳ Do rubbings of leaves in the garden using white paper, crayons, and clipboards.
- ✳ Find and press leaves from the garden or from the trees surrounding your school.

# You Fill Up My Senses

## Concepts

- Plants are made up of many parts.
- Each plant has its own unique look.
- Plants have varied textures.
- Some plants have distinct smells.
- Some plants make noise.
- Some plants are edible.

## Materials

five large trays (such as copy-paper box lids, cookie sheets, cafeteria trays)
colored markers
posterboard strips
plants that make noise
plants with a strong fragrance
plants that can be eaten
plants that are brightly colored
plants that have an interesting texture

## Description

1. Label each tray with a word and picture representing one of the five senses (look, touch, listen, smell, and taste).
2. Ask children to brainstorm garden items that could be displayed on each tray. Work with children in small groups to collect items from the garden for each tray, such as the following:

    Listen:  wind chime, Chinese lanterns, dried gourds, dried money plant, northern sea oats
    Look:    Canterbury bells, zinnias, snapdragons, alyssum, geraniums
    Touch:   lamb's ear, dusty miller, 'autumn joy' sedum, strawflowers, cockscomb, hens and chicks
    Smell:   thyme, sage, basil, chives, cucumber slices
    Taste:   parsley, strawberries, cherry tomatoes, carrots, pansies, nasturtiums

3. Place trays in an area where they can be visited and manipulated by children or guests.
4. Guide children as they explore and encourage them to use their senses as they manipulate the objects.

## Extensions

Assign children to four groups (touch, smell, look, listen). Give each group a clipboard and take a sensory walk through the playground, neighborhood, or nearby park. Encourage the children to find interesting items to write on their list (such as touch the cool gravel or hot asphalt, look for insects, smell food from a nearby restaurant, listen for birds singing). Return to the room and ask each group to report what they found. Post their records for parents to see at the end of the day.

## Seed to Plant Matchup

### Concepts
- Many plants begin as seeds.
- Each seed becomes a specific type of plant.
- Seeds can be identified by size, shape, and color.

### Materials
20 note cards
10 pairs of different seeds
seed catalogs, empty seed packets, or old garden magazines
glue
marker

### Description
1. You will need two seeds each of ten types (for example: pumpkin, corn, pea, tomato, lima bean, sunflower, gourd, watermelon, carrot, and love in a puff), and a picture of the plant produced by each seed. Glue a seed to each of twenty blank note cards, so you have two sets of ten. Set aside one set. Turn the other set over and affix a picture of the plant the seed produces to the opposite side of the card. You will now have one set of cards with a seed on each card, and one set of cards with a seed on one side and the corresponding plant on the other. Write the name of the plant below each picture with a marker. For younger children, offer only five sets of cards at one time.
2. Place the matchup game on the table in the science area during center time with ten cards showing plants and ten cards showing seeds.
3. When children show interest, ask them if they can match the plants to the seeds that they come from without picking up the cards.
4. Once ten pairs have been made, show the child how to turn the cards over to see whether the seeds are identical.

### Extensions
- Take children on a fieldwork trip to the garden section at a local discount or hardware store. While you are there, visit the seed packet rack and select seeds to plant in your garden.
- Harvest seeds from your garden at the end of the season for children to plant at school or home next year.
- Prepare pumpkinseeds or sunflower seeds to eat as a snack.

### Safety Considerations
Read seed packets carefully to be sure that the seeds have not been treated with any potentially harmful chemicals and make sure that the seeds are not toxic. (For instance, angel's trumpet and castor bean seeds are highly toxic.)

## Forever Flowers

### Concepts

- ⊛ Some plants have flowers with petals of different shapes, sizes, and textures.
- ⊛ Flowers can be preserved through drying.
- ⊛ Substances such as sand and cornmeal help the flower hold its shape as it dries.

### Materials

shoebox
fine sand or cornmeal
small funnels
flowers for drying

### Description

1. If you use sand, start with fine, clean, dry sand and sift it through a strainer until you have only the finest particles.
2. Guide the children as they fill the shoebox about 1 inch deep with the drying medium (cornmeal or sand).
3. Remove most of the stem from a flower. Have the children place the flower on top of the drying medium. (Do one flower at a time.)
4. Have a child hold a finger over the tip of the funnel as you fill it with drying medium. Once it is full, show the child how to release her finger and let the sand flow around the flower. (If you don't have a funnel, use a small spoon to gently add the sand.) Try to avoid dumping the sand directly on the flower, but build it up around the sides until it naturally flows over the petals. Your goal is to preserve the shape of the flower by surrounding it with the medium, but don't be too fussy. It is hard for young children to control the medium with precision.
5. Continue adding flowers and surrounding them with the medium until the box is full.
6. Let the box sit for about two weeks. To remove the flowers, *slowly* pour the medium from one corner of the box. As the flowers become visible, remove them with a slotted spoon. Brush off the excess drying medium with a clean paintbrush.

### Extensions

- ⊛ Use sand for one box and cornmeal for the other. Compare the results with the same kind of flower.
- ⊛ Compare the results with different kinds of flowers. Which look the most natural dried? Make notes in your garden journal to refer to next time you dry flowers.

---

### Flowers that dry well in cornmeal or sand

astilbe
black-eyed Susan
butterfly weed

| | |
|---|---|
| delphinium | Queen Anne's lace |
| hollyhock | rose |
| marigold | Shasta daisy |
| peony | snapdragon |
| | stock |
| | yarrow |
| | zinnia |

---

### Flower Preservation

Some flowers, called everlastings, dry easily if you simply gather them together in small bunches, tie the stems with a string or rubber band, and hang them upside down until they are dry. Here are some everlastings you can dry this way:

artemesia
lavender
sweet marjoram

| | |
|---|---|
| tansy | statice |
| yarrow | strawflowers |
| chive blossoms | Chinese lanterns |
| | baby's breath |
| | globe amaranth |

# Pressed for Time

## Concepts

⊛ Each plant has its own identifiable characteristics.

⊛ Plants can be preserved for future study through pressing.

⊛ Plants can be pressed using various methods.

## Materials

waxed paper
old newspapers
two wooden boards (about 16 by 12 inches)
cardboard
sturdy string
or a commercial plant press

## Description

1. Gather flowers and leaves for pressing from the garden. Select these early in the morning, when they are fresh, but the dew has dried. Ask the children if they would like to learn about a way to preserve or save these samples for later use. Gather children around a table where materials are prepared. Explain to the children that they will be learning to preserve plants using a plant press.

2. You can make a plant press by using two wooden boards, newspaper, and cardboard. Start by placing a wooden board on the table. Then place a sheet of newspaper, folded in half, on the board. Open the newspaper and place a plant inside the fold. Fold the newspaper over again and place a sheet of cardboard on top. Repeat with another piece of newspaper and another plant.

3. Continue layering newspaper and cardboard until several flowers and leaves have been inserted. Place the second board on the top. Wrap string around the entire stack, pull until it is tight, and tie a knot.

4. Place the press in a warm, dry place. Wait several days before checking the plants. When the plants are dry, take them out and examine them closely. Engage children in a discussion of how the flower or leaf has changed in the pressing process. Pressed plants can be stored at room temperature between two sheets of newspaper or waxed paper.

## Extensions

⊛ Make your own concentration matching game by pressing two each of ten to fifteen different flowers, herbs, or leaves.

⊛ Use pressed flowers to make greeting cards or garden party invitations. Cut clear Con-Tact paper into pieces larger than the flowers or leaves you have pressed. Peel the backing off the Con-Tact paper and gently place the flower or leaf face down on the sticky side. Then turn the Con-Tact paper over and stick it to a folded piece of construction paper or cardstock. Encourage children to write or dictate a message on the inside of the card.

⊛ Make a book of garden favorites. Have children each select their favorite garden plant and press one leaf or flower from it. Use Con-Tact paper to adhere these to separate sheets of same-size paper. Encourage each child to label the dried sample with invented spelling or copy the name from the garden label, a seed catalog, or a seed packet. Compile these pages and bind as a book. Involve children in selecting a title, creating a cover, and making a title page.

# Dig a Little Deeper

## Concepts

- ⊛ A plant's roots absorb water and minerals from the soil.
- ⊛ Roots hold the plant in the ground.
- ⊛ Lateral roots extend from the main root.
- ⊛ Root growth occurs at the tip of each root where fine root hairs absorb food from the soil.

## Materials

hand trowel
magnifying glasses
pencil and paper or garden journal
various plants from the garden
*Eyewitness Books: Plant* (see appendix 1)

## Description

1. Take children to the garden and help them dig up a few plants to study. Herbs work well for this activity, since they grow abundantly in most gardens. Try digging up a basil plant, a sage plant, and some parsley and mint. For comparison purposes, you might also choose to dig up a radish, a carrot, a potato, some lettuce, and any nearby weeds.
2. Gather a small group of children to study the various plants using magnifying glasses. Engage the children in a discussion of similarities and differences. Call attention to the roots of each plant.
3. Open *Eyewitness Books: Plant* to pages 8 and 9. Have the children examine the plants again to see if they can distinguish between the three types of roots discussed in the book.
4. Take pictures of these plants and their roots for your garden journal. Have children choose one plant to draw and encourage them to draw the plant as it looks both above and below the ground.

## Extensions

- ⊛ Give children rulers and let them measure the roots of various plants.
- ⊛ Find and prepare a recipe that calls for fresh gingerroot, such as beef stir-fry.
- ⊛ Use toothpicks to suspend a clove of garlic, a piece of sweet potato or potato, or an avocado pit in a glass of water with the top sticking out. Watch and take notes as the plant develops roots. Then plant it in a pot of soil until it can later be transplanted into your garden.

# Crushed Kaleidoscope

## Concepts

- Each plant has leaves with distinct shapes.
- Leaves contain chlorophyll.
- Leaves have veins.
- Flower petals contain pigment, which gives them their color.

## Materials

green leaves or bright-colored flowers
hammer or a medium-size rock with at least one smooth side
an old blanket
old white or beige-colored sheet
a piece of wood (at least 12 by 12 inches in size)
two tacks or pushpins
permanent marker

## Description

1. Place the old blanket on the ground near the garden and gather a small group of children who are interested in making leaf prints. Invite each child to go into the garden and carefully select one leaf or flower to print. When selecting flowers, remember that simple, circular flowers such as pansies, nasturtiums, or cosmos work best. Supervise the children as they do this, helping them take one leaf or flower without harming the plant. You may want to encourage children to each select a different plant to add variety to the mural and to prevent the overpruning of any one plant.

2. Bring children back together on the blanket. Place the piece of wood on the blanket. Have one child place a leaf or flower on the wooden surface and cover it with a portion of the sheet. Demonstrate how to fasten the sheet into place by using a tack at each of the top corners. This will keep the sheet from slipping about and should provide a clear print. Explain that you will be removing these tacks in a few minutes so they do not need to be pushed completely into the wood.

3. Ask the first child to put on the safety goggles. Hand the child the hammer or stone and let her pound on the leaf or flower. Encourage the child to pound all around the plant in an even manner. Then have her write the name of the plant under the print with a permanent marker.

4. Lift the sheet, without removing the tacks, to make sure the print has transferred to the cloth. If necessary, replace the sheet and continue pounding.

5. Carefully remove the tacks when finished. Have the child hold up the sheet for the others to see. Ask the children to describe the details they see in the print and what made the colors

you see on the sheet. Explain that a pigment called "chlorophyll" gives plants their green color. Tell them that chlorophyll helps plants make energy from sunlight. After printing a flower, explain that pigment gives flower petals their color as well. Add other vocabulary words to the discussion as necessary.

6. Shift the position of the sheet to make a new print on a clean area. Repeat this process with another child and another plant. Continue until all children have had a turn or until the sheet is evenly covered with prints.

7. Display this cloth mural by posting it in the hallway, on a bulletin board, or in another visible place.

## Extensions

Cut up another sheet or use scraps of fabric to let children make individual prints. Sort leaf prints by the number of points on each leaf. Arrange leaf prints by size, from the smallest to the largest. Select some prints to include in your garden journal. Have children tell why they selected each plant for inclusion in the journal, research these plants, and write details about the plants in the journal.

## Safety Considerations

You will need to closely supervise the pounding of the plants to make sure that no one is injured. Have children and teachers wear safety goggles during this portion of the activity.

## Exploring What Plants Need to Grow

### Soiled Again!

#### Concepts

- Plants need soil to grow.
- People can make soil for plants by mixing various materials.
- Some materials are good for plants because they provide moisture and/or nutrients.

#### Materials

large container for mixing soil (for example, sensory table, washtub, or wheelbarrow)
smaller container for measuring soil (for example, bucket or cup measure)
topsoil
peat moss
perlite
water

#### Description

1. Have children explore the three ingredients for the soil. Compare textures, color, and other attributes.
2. Mix in the large container 1 part each of the topsoil, peat moss, and perlite. (So that you can adapt the activity to the size of your container, we have listed the ingredients in parts instead of in quantities. You may want to use measuring cups if you are just making enough soil for a few pots, or you can use buckets or flowerpots if you are making a large quantity of soil.)
3. Add water until the mixture is moistened. At this point, you might want to leave the potting soil out for a few days for the children to explore in the sensory table.
4. Use the soil mixture in pots or in the garden.

#### Extensions

- Add water to each ingredient separately before mixing. Compare the absorption rates of the different media.
- Add soil polymers to the mix. (These are water-absorbing crystals that will help your soil retain moisture. They can be found in nurseries and garden centers.) Put a tablespoon of the dry polymers in a clear container, such as a plastic jar, and fill with water. Observe as the polymers absorb the water. (This should take about thirty minutes.) Compare the size of the polymers before and after the water was added. Add the soil polymers to the soil mixture. (If you are making a lot of soil, you might want to increase the amount of polymers used. The container should help you determine how much you need.)

#### Safety Considerations

Be sure children do not put materials in their mouths. Be extra cautious about this if you use soil polymers because they absorb large quantities of water and should not be ingested. Do not use any materials to which chemical fertilizer has been added.

# Making the Most of Compost

## Concepts

- Plants need food to grow.
- Plants decompose over time and turn into rich compost that can be used to help other plants grow.
- Food scraps can also be used to make compost for the garden.
- Decomposing plants generate heat.

## Materials

rectangular laundry basket
utility knife (to be used by adult only)
hand trowels
soil
compost materials, such as dry leaves, grass clippings, garden clippings, vegetable and fruit scraps, dryer lint, coffee grounds, and eggshells

## Description

1. Use a utility knife to cut out the bottom of the laundry basket.
2. Select an area in or near your garden. Guide the children in digging a hole that is the right size for the laundry basket to sit in. Dig down 4 to 6 inches.
3. Place the laundry basket in the hole. Have the children add a layer of compost materials about 4 inches deep. Sprinkle with a layer of soil. Repeat the layering until you have used up all your compost materials or the basket is full. (If your basket is not full, you can continue adding to it during the next few weeks.)
4. Wet the pile with water. To maintain the compost pile, stir it up periodically. Because of its small size, children should be able to do this with hand cultivators. Also keep the pile moist, but not flooded. When the organic matter has turned brown and crumbly, you have compost.

## Extensions

- Build two compost piles. Put different ingredients in each one and compare the results. Does one kind of organic matter break down more quickly than the other? Do they look the same?
- Build two compost piles, one in the sun and one in the shade. Add the same ingredients to each. Do they take the same amount of time to decompose?
- Take the temperature of the compost pile and graph it. Compost produces heat. How does the temperature in the compost pile compare to the air temperature? Let the children put their hands in the pile and feel the heat.

## Safety Considerations

Some people worry that compost will attract rats. This shouldn't be a problem, so long as you avoid adding meat or dairy products to your compost. Snakes are sometimes attracted to the warmth of a compost pile, but are usually harmless. If you live in an area where snakes are in residence, keep an eye out for them.

# Stinky Tea

## Concepts

- Plants need nutrients to grow.
- Nutrients can come from other plants.
- Heat from the sun makes plants break down into nutrients faster.
- Decomposing matter often has a strong odor.

## Materials

alfalfa pellets (available from feed stores)
water
large container with lid (should hold at least 5 gallons)

## Description

1. Guide the children in selecting a sunny spot for your alfalfa tea to brew. Place your container in this spot.
2. Examine the alfalfa pellets. Discuss their shape. Smell them. Break them apart and examine the texture.
3. Have the children put some alfalfa pellets in the container. Use about 1 cup of alfalfa pellets for every 3 gallons of water the container holds. (You don't have to have exact amounts, so don't worry.)
4. Fill the container with water.
5. Cover the container with the lid and let it sit in the sun. Check the tea each day. Observe the appearance and the smell. It will take about two weeks for the tea to brew. You will know it is finished when it smells really bad. If it doesn't stink, it isn't ready yet. Once it is done, dip it out and put it on the plants. They love stinky alfalfa tea.

## Extensions

- There are many organic fertilizers you can buy that children can put on the garden. Check your garden center to find a selection of cottonseed meal, fish meal, bonemeal, Epsom salts, and others. These can be applied dry by broadcasting around the plants. Other fertilizers need to be mixed with water. Fish emulsion fertilizer is a good choice because it won't burn the plants, even if children spill it on the leaves, and it smells terrible, which never fails to delight young children.
- Record observations of the tea as it brews.
- Compare the growth of a plant that is fertilized with alfalfa tea to a plant that is not. Start with two plants that are the same size and growing under the same conditions. Feed alfalfa tea to one and give no fertilizer to the other. What happens?
- If you have access to fresh manure, you can make manure tea instead of alfalfa tea. Follow the same procedure, except substitute manure for the alfalfa. Since manure often has weed seeds in it, you might want to wrap the manure in burlap or cheesecloth and tie the cloth with string before adding it to the water. This will keep the seeds out of your garden.

*Note: Never put fresh manure directly in your garden. It will burn your plants.*

## Safety Considerations

Five-gallon buckets work well for making alfalfa or manure tea. However, these buckets have been implicated in drowning deaths of toddlers. If you use a 5-gallon bucket, be sure it is in an area where it is not accessible to children unless they are under close adult supervision (outside the playground fence, for instance).

# Feeling Fine

## Concepts

⊛ Soil is made up of different substances that help plants grow.

⊛ Some substances in soil hold water for the plants.

⊛ Some substances in soil help water drain.

## Materials

sensory table or large tub
growing medium, such as peat moss, perlite, sand, clay, topsoil
water
hand tools, such as trowels and cultivators
buckets or other containers

## Description

1. Use only one type of growing medium at a time, so children can explore the specific characteristics of that material. Fill the sensory table or tub with the medium.
2. Add water, as needed. For materials such as perlite and peat moss, which contain dust, be sure to add water so the children don't inhale the dust. Other substances, such as topsoil, sand, and clay, can be explored both wet and dry.
3. Allow the children to explore the materials with their hands and with tools. Ask questions that encourage thinking and observation, helping them determine whether the substance holds or repels water and how water effects the material.
4. After children have explored one type of medium, remove it and try another.

## Extensions

Use several tubs containing different materials so that children can compare the textures and properties.

## Safety Considerations

Be sure that children do not put materials in their mouths.

# Mulch Madness

## Concepts

- Adding a layer of mulch after planting helps soil to retain moisture.
- Adding a layer of mulch after planting helps to control weed growth.
- Many materials may be used as mulch.
- The effectiveness of mulch varies by the material used.

## Materials

seedlings
soil
shovels or hand trowels
newspaper
straw
wood chips
grass clippings
coffee grounds
cloth scraps
black plastic
water
measuring cups or watering can
sprinkler
handheld rulers

## Description

1. Send a note home with the children asking parents to save and donate grass clippings, coffee grounds, cloth scraps, and old newspapers.
2. Select seedlings and plant them in your garden or choose an area of your existing garden that has been weeded, but not mulched, for this activity. Water the seedlings evenly. For a large space, use a sprinkler to do this. For a container garden with containers that are similar in size, use measuring cups or a small watering can to add the same amount of water to each container.
3. Allow children to explore various materials used for mulching. Try layered newspaper, with holes cut to fit around each seedling. Collect and try traditional wood chips, straw, grass clippings, coffee grounds, black plastic, and cloth scraps. Encourage children to come up with their own creative ideas to try.
4. Demonstrate to children how to apply mulch around, not on top of, a seedling. Divide the garden in even sections. Have children select and apply one type of mulch to each section. Explain that this experiment works best if the thickness of the mulch is about the same in each section. Give kids handheld rulers to measure the depth of their mulch material as they apply it.
5. Work with children to make a sketch of the garden, recording the type of mulch used in each section.
6. Remind the children to monitor the amount of moisture in each section on a daily basis to determine which types of mulch are the most effective in holding water.

7. Help the children to watch for weeds and count the number in each section. After two weeks, create a graph showing the types of mulch used and the number of weeds in each corresponding section.
8. Discuss the results with the children and encourage them to draw some conclusions or repeat the experiment to test the accuracy of their results.

## Extensions
Use a field guide to identify the weeds you find in the garden. Make a weed journal by pressing weeds and attaching them to the pages with Con-Tact paper. Then add factual information and children's dictation about each weed.

## Safety Considerations
If children use shovels to apply mulch materials, supervise closely to prevent injury to other children and to plants.

## Measuring Up

### Concepts

- ⊛ Plants need water to live.
- ⊛ Rainfall can be measured with a rain gauge.
- ⊛ Rain gauges come in various sizes and styles.
- ⊛ Rainfall can be charted on a line graph.

### Materials

2 to 3 rain gauges of various sizes and styles
chart paper or garden journal
markers

### Description

Preparation—Before you start this activity, you'll need to purchase or borrow two to three styles and sizes of rain gauges (fence mount, ground mount, large easy-to-read numbers, and so on).

1. Place the gauges at various locations around the garden. Have the children help. Teach the children not to disturb or empty the gauges during play time, so that an accurate measure can be taken.
2. Encourage the children to check these gauges daily. Assist the children by demonstrating how to read the water level. Compare the water level in each gauge to see if they each measured the same amount of rainfall. Then show the children how to empty each gauge so that it is ready to measure the next rainfall.
3. Chart rainfall in a garden journal or on chart paper for two to four weeks. If it does not rain, encourage children to observe the effect of dryness on the plants. Describe this in the garden journal before asking children to assist in watering the garden.
4. Use a sprinkler to water the garden, if you continue to have no rain. Check the rain gauges to see if the sprinkler is watering evenly.

### Extensions

Plan a walk for a rainy day. Send a note to parents asking them to send boots, jackets, and umbrellas with the children. If there are not enough umbrellas, you can always gather children under a large sheet of plastic (tarp, drop cloth, tablecloth) with a teacher on each end. On the first rainy day, adjust your plans and take a walk. Encourage the children to notice the sound, smell, and feel of the rain. Sing songs about rainy weather, such as "Rain, Rain, Go Away," or, "It's Raining, It's Pouring," as you walk. Upon return to the classroom, take dictation from the children about the experience, including their guesses as to how much rain will be in the gauges. When the rain stops, take them outside to check their predictions.

# Exploring Garden Creatures

## Slippery When Wet

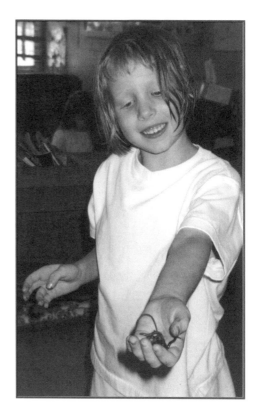

*Concepts*
- Worms need moisture to live.
- Worms will move toward moisture.

*Materials*
earthworms
paper towels
large pan with a shallow rim
water

*Description*
1. Have the children wet some paper towels so that they are damp, but not dripping. Spread them so that they cover half the pan. Next, place a dry paper towel so that the edges of the wet and dry towels touch.
2. Put a worm on one of the towels, next to the touching edges. Observe the worm. Talk about where it goes and what it does. Does it stay on or move to one of the towels?
3. Take the worm off and repeat with another worm. This time, start the worm on the other side. (For instance, if you started the first worm on the wet side, start this one on the dry side.) Discuss what happens.

*Extensions*
- Record your results on a graph, with one side labeled "wet" and the other "dry." Mark which side each worm prefers. Compare the results.
- Try using many worms at once. Put five on the wet towel and five on the dry towel. Count how many are on each towel after five minutes.

*Safety Considerations*
The main safety issue in worm experiments is for the worm. If we are to expose children to living creatures, we must model respect. Young children need to be closely supervised while handling fragile living beings, such as worms. Be careful not to leave the worms out so long that the paper dries out, because the worms will too.

# Rulers of the Deep

## Concepts

- ⊛ Worms eat paper as well as food that we might otherwise throw away.
- ⊛ Worms need moisture to live.
- ⊛ As the food passes through their bodies, the worms turn it into castings, which are rich in nutrients that plants like.
- ⊛ We must care for the worms, adding food and moisture periodically, so that they remain healthy.

## Materials

large shallow container (8 to 12 inches deep), such as a storage box or galvanized washtub
shredded paper or newspaper
a cup of soil
water
1 pound redworms (Purchase redworms, or red wigglers, for your worm composter from sources listed in the section on garden creatures in appendix 3. Do not substitute another type of worm, since they may have very specific requirements that you will not be able to meet.)

## Description

1. Have the children fill the container with shredded paper.
2. Guide the children as they add water, a cup at a time, until the paper is evenly moistened. It should be thoroughly damp, but water should not sit in the bottom of the container. This mixture is called worm bedding.
3. Add the cup of soil. This will help the worms digest the paper.
4. Investigate the worms with the children. They will probably want to hold and examine them. Take lots of time for this step. Show the children how to gently handle the worms by holding their hands flat and letting the worms crawl on the palm. Look closely at the worms. Notice the small band (clitellum) around one end. Discuss how the worms feel.
5. Place the worms in the box. Cover it lightly with a sheet of heavy plastic or the lid to the container. (If you use an unventilated lid, drill a few holes in it so the worms will get oxygen.)
6. Your worms will be fine for a while because they will eat the paper, but the children will soon want to add food scraps for the worms to eat. You can feed the worms vegetable and fruit scraps or leftovers, eggshells and leftover bread or cereal products. Avoid milk or meat products, as these will draw pests. When the children add food to the composter, have them bury it under some of the paper. Rotate the area where you bury the food so you are putting it in a different spot each time.
7. Keep the compost moist. The vegetation you feed will add some moisture, so don't overdo it. A good way to add moisture is to let the children spray water with a spray bottle.
8. Remove the worms, if you want to continue using them, when you notice that much of your bedding has turned into castings, which are dark and fine. (Alternatively, you can put the whole mixture, worms included, in the garden.) To sort the worms from the compost, put small piles of compost on a large sheet of plastic. Shine a bright light on each pile. The worms will crawl away from the light toward the middle of the pile. (This takes a while, but children love it.) Gradually scrape the compost off the pile, giving the worms plenty of time to flee. You should eventually be left with a ball of worms. Use the compost for your garden and start a new box for the worms.

Note—Chant the worm-sorting song to hurry the process along:

*Worms, worms, run from the light.*
*Worms, worms, get out of sight.*

## Safety Considerations

Always have the children wash their hands before and after handling the worms or compost materials.

# Who's Afraid of the Dark?

## Concepts

- Worms prefer dark to light.
- Worms move away from the light.

## Materials

earthworms
pan or box with shallow sides (a cake pan is a good choice)
cardboard or dark paper
paper towels
water

## Description

1. Have the children dampen the paper towels and line the entire bottom of the box or pan with them.
2. Cover half of the box or pan by resting dark paper or cardboard on the sides of the pan or box to keep out the light. Leave the other half uncovered.
3. Put a worm in the middle of the box. Observe and discuss what you see. Where does the worm go?
4. When you are satisfied this worm has decided where it wants to be, put it back in its home and try the experiment with another worm. Does it do the same thing?

## Extensions

- Record your results on a graph, with one side labeled "light" and the other side labeled "dark." Mark the side each worm prefers. Compare the results.
- Try using many worms at once. Put them so that they are both in the dark and in the light. Count how many are in the light and how many are in the dark in five minutes.

## Safety Considerations

See safety concern under the activity "Slippery When Wet."

# A Touching Experience

## Concepts

- Worms respond to touch.
- Some parts of a worm's body are more sensitive to touch than others.
- The banded area of the worm is called the clitellum (klih-TEL-um).

## Materials

earthworms
moist paper towel

## Description

1. Place the worm on the moist paper towel. Observe it for a minute and discuss what it does.
2. Very gently, touch the worm on its head, in the middle, and then on its tail. (The worm's tail is the pointed end. The head is closest to the banded area, which is called the clitellum.)
3. Talk about which parts of the worm move most actively when touched. Which move the least?
4. Repeat several times with different worms to see if you get the same results.

## Extensions

Record your results on a graph. One way to do this is to divide the graph into three sections labeled "head," "middle," and "tail." For each worm, mark which part responds most actively to touch. Compare your results for several worms.

## Safety Considerations

See safety concern under the activity "Slippery When Wet."

# Birdwatching Backpack

## Concepts

- Birds can be identified by their size, shape, color, and behavior.
- Birds can be attracted with food, shelter, and water.
- Certain birds live in certain regions of the country.
- Male and female birds of the same species are often different colors.

## Materials

backpack or other small bag with handles
small field guide with color photos or sketches (see the list of field guides in the appendices)
plastic tweezers
magnifying glasses
ruler or small tape measure
colored pencils
sketchpad or small unlined notebook
plastic zipper storage bags of various sizes
binoculars (child- or adult-size)

## Description

1. Gather the above materials and place them in the backpack or other portable container.
2. Meet with children in small groups to introduce the backpack, discuss the idea of observing birds on the playground, and demonstrate the use of the materials in the kit. Allow children time to practice focusing the binoculars, picking up small objects carefully with the tweezers, and measuring the length of common classroom items using the ruler or tape measure.
3. Show the field guide to the children and explain that this book will help them to learn about the birds they see outdoors. Show and explain key features of the book, such as regional maps and drawings or photographs. Ask the children to name a bird they have seen on the playground. Use the index to locate the number of the page that describes this bird. Read the text to the children. Then call attention to the key information given about this bird, such as the size, physical characteristics, behavior, diet, song, and the differences between males and females.
4. Tell the children that the storage bags can be used to store and protect feathers, fallen nests, or empty eggshells found on walks or on the playground. Explain that the colored pencils and sketchbook can be used to record as many details about the bird as possible, such as colors, specific markings, and other key features.
5. Explain that the birdwatching backpack will be available at all outdoor times and that children may use it freely as long as they return all of the materials to the backpack before returning indoors. (You may want to enclose a laminated, illustrated list of all items that should be in the bag.) Talk to the children about how to sit quietly near the garden, birdbath, or feeders and wait for birds to visit.
6. At the next scheduled outdoor play time, remind the children about the backpack (depending on the size of your group and the children's level of interest, you may want to have a sign-up sheet to assist in turn-taking and use of the backpack). Remember that birds are more active and, therefore, more likely to be seen, early in the day. Keeping your feeders full and your birdbath fresh will likely attract more birds. You may want to discuss this with the children and encourage them to take responsibility for monitoring and maintenance of the feeders and birdbath.

7. Assist children as necessary with use of the field guide, recording important data, labeling sketches, and drawing conclusions. As you observe birds with the children, call attention to bird behavior. Is the bird hopping, walking, or running? Does it climb up a tree trunk or work down the tree headfirst? Does it eat from the feeder or probe the ground for worms? Teach children to use the field guide to incorporate this information into the identification process.

8. Discuss their observations at small or large group times over the next few weeks.

## Extensions

- Plan a visit to the bird section of a local pet store or a local bird refuge to study, sketch, and observe various types of birds.
- Collect a variety of bird feathers. Using a reference book or field guide, sort the feathers into the four main types: down feathers, body feathers, tail feathers, and wing feathers.
- After becoming familiar with the birds common to your region, create a chart showing the birds you have observed in your garden or near your playground. Hang the chart outdoors or take it outside each time you go to the playground. Encourage children to make a tally mark next to each species of bird when they see one visit the schoolyard. After one week, total the tally marks and discuss the results.
- Build birdfeeders out of wood, pop bottles, and other recycled materials to hang in the garden.
- Experiment with various types of bird food to see if you can attract new species of birds to your garden.
- Collect fallen bird nests after a storm to study under a magnifying glass in the classroom. Note the types of materials used in building the nest. Read about how various birds build their nests in a nonfiction reference book such as *Eyewitness Books: Bird* (see appendix 1). Place small scraps of yarn, string, tissue paper, or cloth in a small box near the feeder. Watch to see if birds take some of these materials to use in building their nests.

## Safety Considerations

Avoid disturbing birds while watching them. Be extra careful when observing parent birds with their young. Always require children to wash their hands thoroughly after handling feathers, nests, eggshells, or dead birds.

# Critter Hunting

## Concepts

- Earthworms burrow into the ground by swallowing soil as they move.
- Earthworms, pill bugs, sow bugs, and ants need moisture to live.
- Pill bugs and sow bugs are arthropods, but not insects.
- Pill bugs will roll up to protect themselves, while sow bugs will run away.

## Materials

shovel or hand trowel
containers for collecting critters
shallow trays or pans for observation
magnifying glasses
paper and pencils
reference books, such as
> *Golden Guide: Insects* (New York: St. Martin's Press, 2001)
> *Insect* by Laurence Mound (New York: Knopf, 1990)
> *Earthworms, Dirt, and Rotten Leaves* by Molly McLaughlin. (New York: Atheneum, 1986)

*Compost Critters* by Bianca Lavies (New York: Dutton, 1993)
*Earthworm* by Andrienne Soutter-Perrot (American Education Publishing, 1994)

## Description

1. Ask the children if they would like to go outside and look for critters on the playground or in the garden. Have them chart their predictions of the critters they think they might find and where they might look.
2. Go outside and look in some of the places suggested. If no critters are found, try looking in damp places, underneath rocks or boards, in rotting logs or cement cracks, and in piles of damp rubbish. You will likely find sow bugs and pill bugs, as well as earthworms. Earthworms may also be found on wet sidewalks, just after a rain, or by digging directly into your garden soil. Smaller worms should be near the soil's surface, with larger worms living much deeper. Try digging down about 6 to 12 inches with a shovel or hand trowel, if you can do so without disturbing your plants.
3. You might also want to search for ant trails and follow them to see if you can find the colony. Anthills can often be found on loose, dry soil. If you find anthills, be sure to teach children to avoid stepping on the ants or disturbing them. Explain that the hill is the ants' home and no one wants their home to be ruined.
4. Once you have located some critters, carefully collect a few of each type to study for the day. Place a homemade critter container, such as a baby-food jar with small holes in the lid on the ground near the critters and scoop them up.
5. Take these critters to the classroom, a nearby picnic table, or a blanket on the ground for observation. Often it is helpful to take some of the critter's natural habitat with you, such as a piece of rotting bark, some wet leaves, or a chunk of wet soil. Overwhelmed critters may want to hide and observing this behavior will add to the learning experience. Worms, sow bugs, and pill bugs can be held safely when placed in the flat, open hand of a child.
6. At the observation area, you may want to remove the critters from their containers and place them in several shallow trays for observation. Old cafeteria trays or cookie sheets work well for this, as do shoebox lids. Encourage the children to observe with magnifying glasses.

7. Give the children paper and pencils to record what they observe. If you are working outside on a blanket, give children clipboards or large flat books to place under their paper so that writing and drawing is easier. This type of documentation can also take place directly into a garden journal.

8. Ask children to note key aspects such as body parts, color, appearance, and behavior. This will encourage children to observe carefully. Older children can choose two different critters to compare, such as sow bugs and pill bugs. Take dictation for children who do not yet write using invented spelling.

9. Provide children with reference books and encourage them to find and read books about the critters they are observing. Some of this information can be shared with peers and added to their drawings.

10. Release all critters back into their original surroundings by the end of the same day to preserve their life and the natural environment around your school. Be sure that all their needs are met while they are in your care. For instance, if you do not provide moisture in the form of damp paper towels or soil, worms may dry out. Paying attention to the needs of creatures like these and returning them to their natural habitat teaches children to respect living things.

## Extensions

- At circle time, have children use their bodies to dramatically represent for the rest of the group the critters they observed.
- Start an earthworm compost box in your classroom.
- Help children make critter containers to take home by assisting them as they use a hammer and nail to poke small holes in the lids of recycled margarine or whipped cream containers.

## Safety Considerations

Supervise children closely to make sure they do not disturb insects that might cause them harm, such as bees, wasps, or biting ants. Supervise children using shovels very closely and remind them to keep the shovel down near the ground. Avoid removing ants from their critter containers if observing them indoors, since they might escape into your classroom. Glass baby-food jars can break if dropped and should be closely supervised. Avoid sending glass jars home with children.

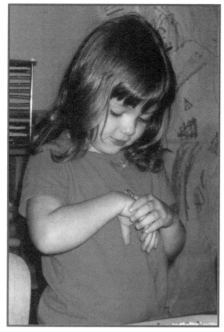

# Up Close and Personal with Insects

## Concepts

- Insects are arthropods.
- The life cycle of an insect is called metamorphosis.
- Egg, larvae, pupa, and adult are the stages of metamorphosis.
- Insects have six legs.
- Each insect has a hard exoskeleton covering all parts of its body.
- Each order, or group, of insects has its own unique characteristics.
- Butterflies and ladybugs are beneficial to plants.
- The body of an insect has three divisions: head, thorax, and abdomen.

## Materials

insect eggs or larvae (Ladybugs, butterflies, and ants are good subjects to study because they will likely be visible in your garden at one time or another. Ladybug or butterfly eggs or larvae can be ordered from educational supply catalogs, such as Insectlore or Lakeshore. Ant farms are readily available from a variety of sources.)

transparent insect container with holes in the lid or a mesh cage

magnifying glasses

paper and colored pencils or crayons

preferred food of the selected insect (such as fresh leaves, live plants, fresh fruit, cotton balls soaked with sugar water, or honey)

reference books (see appendix 1)

## Description

1. Read through all instructions carefully and research the needs of the insect before beginning the project. Make plans in advance for how and when the insects will be released into the environment. This will affect the timing of your project. For example, releasing live insects into the outdoors would be inappropriate in a cold winter climate. Remember that one of your goals should be to teach children respect for all living things.
2. Once the insects arrive, introduce the project to the children. Follow all directions with great care to be sure your insects live to adulthood.
3. Be sure to surround the children with many informational resources throughout the life of the project, as they will be motivated to learn everything they can about these live visitors. Consider locating several fiction and nonfiction library books, Web site addresses, posters, and three-dimensional insect models. Research how the insect interacts with plant life. Is it harmful or helpful? What types of plants does it prefer?
4. Place the insect container in a safe place at children's eye level. A sturdy shelf or table works well. Some butterfly-net cages need to be hung from the ceiling. Choose an area of the classroom that is relatively calm, such as the reading or science area.
5. Place magnifying glasses near the container and provide time each day for children to observe the development of the insects in small groups. One way to do this is to place just enough chairs in the area for the number of children it can safely hold. Allowing too many children to crowd around the cage may lead to accidents. You don't want to see the ant farm fall to the floor with ants crushed or quickly escaping.

6. Place several journals or clipboards with paper and writing utensils near the insect container. This will foster documentation of metamorphosis. Hang posters showing the four stages of the insect life cycle and the parts of the insect nearby. Provide vocabulary to children as appropriate, taking advantage of each teachable moment. Record children's comments or encourage them to use invented spelling to write down key information or label artwork. Children's drawings will become more detailed as they gain more and more factual knowledge about the selected insect.

7. Ask children to share their observations at circle or large group time each day. Ask the group, "What's going on with the ladybugs today?" or, "Has anyone noticed anything different about the caterpillars?" Take down children's dictation, date it, and post it near the insect container.

8. Learn alongside the children. Don't be afraid to admit that you don't know all the details. Emphasize your own curiosity and model for children how to find answers to hard questions.

## Safety Considerations

For the safety of your insects, teach children never to shake, move, or bang on the container—especially if it is made of glass. In addition, teach children to leave the lid on the container at all times so insects do not escape into your classroom. Explain to the children that it is better for the insects to stay in the container until it is time for them to be released into the outdoors where they belong.

# Calling All Ants!

## Concepts
- Ants collect food and transport it to their nest.
- Ants prefer some foods to others.
- Ants are insects and insects are arthropods.

## Materials
shoebox lid or large, flat piece of cardboard
baby-food jar or lid
marker
various foods, such as jelly, syrup, small bits of meat, granulated sugar, a slice of lime, crumbled crackers, shredded cheese, and so on
books about ants (see book list in appendix 1)

## Description
1. Using the baby-food jar and marker, have the children trace six circles onto the box lid or cardboard.
2. Have the children fill each circle with a different type of food. Ask the children to predict which food they think will be the ants' favorite and why. Take dictation on a chart or in a garden journal.
3. Take the cardboard or lid into the garden, and with the children, place it where it will not be disturbed by children or noticed by birds. You might want to interview children to find out where they have previously spotted ants or anthills in the garden and place it in that location.
4. Encourage the children to leave the area and allow ants to notice the food. Meanwhile, read several books about ants and arthropods.
5. Return at one-hour intervals to check the progress of the ants and notice their activity. Encourage the children to observe which foods are preferred and which, if any, are undisturbed.
6. Use a field guide on insects to identify the type of ants you attract.
7. Revisit the site many times throughout the day to track progress, check children's predictions, and draw conclusions about preferred foods.

## Extensions
- Encourage the children to draw pictures of the harvesting ants. Take dictation about the process.
- Ask the children for other food suggestions and repeat the process several days in a row. You might even try putting out larger items (such as a whole graham cracker, half an apple, or a slice of cheese) to see how it affects the harvest. Chart and compare the results as you go.

## Safety Considerations
Discourage children from disturbing the ants as they harvest. Some ants do bite.

# One Step at a Time

## Concepts

- Stepping-stones show us where to walk in the garden.
- People often add decorations to their gardens.

## Materials

dishpan or other container for mixing concrete
concrete mix
water
trowel
gloves
mold (You can purchase a concrete mold or use a plastic storage
    container. Size and shape can vary, but you'll want the finished stone to be about 3 inches
    deep.)
vegetable oil
decorations such as ceramic pieces, shells, marbles, glass globules, buttons, stones

## Description

1. Have the children grease the mold by coating it lightly with vegetable oil. This will make it easier to get the stone out later.
2. Put concrete mix in dishpan. The amount you need will depend on the size of your stone. Don't worry about getting it exact; you can make more if you need it. (Have the children stand back while you pour the concrete so they won't breathe the dust.)
3. Have the children add water a little bit at a time, mixing it in gently with the trowel. Add just enough water to dampen the concrete thoroughly. It should be dry enough that you can form a ball with it.
4. Fill the mold with the concrete mixture. Bang the mold a few times on a solid surface to help release air bubbles. Have the children level the top with the trowel.
5. Let the children decorate the top of the stone with the objects you have selected.
6. Let the stone dry for three days before removing it from the mold.

*Note: Large stones should be reinforced with a layer of hardware cloth or chicken wire. Cut it about 1 inch smaller than the mold. Put about 1 inch of concrete in the mold, lay down the wire and then fill the mold the rest of the way.*

## Extensions

Have children make individual stepping-stones with their names, handprints, and other small objects. Then use them to make a pathway through or to the garden.

## Safety Considerations

- Be careful not to breathe in the concrete dust.
- Adults and children should wear gloves when handling the concrete, as it can be irritating to the skin.
- Children who are still consistently putting sensory materials in their mouths should not participate in this activity.

# Sunflower Heights

We noticed that our sunflowers were growing very tall. One day we decided to measure the tallest sunflower to see how tall it was. Sara got on the ladder and measured the sunflower. Maggie held the tape at the bottom. The sunflower was ten feet tall.

Next, we measured a long piece of paper and cut it so that it was ten feet long—as tall as the sunflower. We brought in another sunflower that had broken off in the wind so that we could examine the details for our drawing.

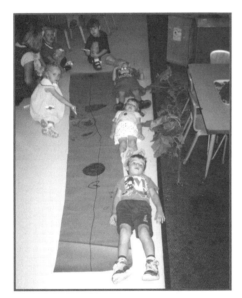

We drew the sunflower head first, carefully studying the head of the real sunflower, so it would look just right. We noticed that the center, where the seeds grow, is brown, and the surrounding petals are yellow. Next we drew the stem and the leaves. Maggie noticed that the leaves are toothed, and she carefully made a zigzag edge to her sunflower leaf.

Finally, we wondered how tall the sunflower was compared to us. We guessed how many children it would take to be as tall as the sunflower. Then we measured the children against the sunflower. The sunflower was as tall as three preschoolers.

## Learning and Development

The children worked on observing and describing the sunflower and the relationships of its parts. They represented the sunflower through drawing, exploring the relationship between pictures and real objects. They worked on math concepts by measuring the sunflower, both with conventional means of measurement and with less conventional means (their own bodies), which was more meaningful to them. They studied spatial relationships, observing the erect sunflower and comparing it to the sunflower that had broken off and was lying on the floor.

# How Big?

Measuring plants can become a regular part of your garden project as you study the growth of plants.

## Concepts

* Plants continue to grow throughout their lives.
* We can find out how much a plant has grown by measuring it.

## Materials

1 tall plant to measure (sunflower, corn, hollyhocks)
ladder (if plant is too tall for teacher to reach the top)
tape measure
roll of paper
markers
flowers and/or leaves from another plant of the same variety (such as another sunflower or hollyhock plant)

## Description

1. Gather together by the plant you've selected. While a child holds the end of the tape measure, the teacher should determine the height of the plant, using the ladder if necessary.
2. Roll out the paper and measure a distance, equal to the height of the plant, on the paper. Cut the paper at that length.
3. Show the children the leaves and flowers from the other plant. Encourage them to examine the two closely. Talk about things you observe, such as any visible seeds, the shape and color of the petals, the shape of the leaves, and so on.
4. Have the children draw the plant life-size on the long paper.
5. After the work is complete, measure the plant with people or objects from the classroom. How many children does it take to equal the height of the plant? How many blocks? How many baby dolls? Try a number of different objects and write your results on the paper or an accompanying chart.

6. Display your representation of the plant and your conclusions. (Our sunflower ended up being taller than the wall and we had to bend it over onto the ceiling. We added to our list of conclusions, "The sunflower is taller than the wall.")

## Extensions

* Since children don't have any special understanding of inches and feet or of metrics, you can use anything to measure. For small plants, Unifix cubes work well. Children can chart the growth of a plant from week to week by measuring with the cubes, then draw around the cubes on a graph to come up with a visual representation of the plant's growth. For bigger plants, you can use other familiar objects from the classroom, such as unit blocks, to measure.
* Compare the size of different varieties of flowers. For instance, compare the size of a 'Russian Mammoth' sunflower to a smaller variety.
* Represent a number of small and large flowers this way. Label each flower. Make a wall collage by pasting the representations side-by-side.

# For the Birds

## Concepts

- Birds need water to drink and bathe.
- People can attract birds by providing them with fresh water.
- A birdbath is an effective way to provide fresh water for birds.

## Materials

washtub or other large container for mixing concrete

32-gallon plastic garbage can with lid (with straight sides so the birdbath will be easy to remove)

concrete mix

water hose (attached to water source)

trowels

gloves

old tire

vegetable oil

chicken wire or hardware cloth cut about 1 inch smaller than the garbage-can lid

decorations such as ceramic pieces, shells, marbles, glass globules, buttons, stones

## Description

1. Have the children coat the inside of the garbage-can lid with vegetable oil. This will make the birdbath easier to remove. An alternative is to line the lid with plastic.
2. Have the children place the garbage-can lid inside the tire so it sits level. If you don't have a tire, you can dig a hole in the ground or in the sandbox to hold the garbage-can lid level.
3. Pour concrete into the washtub. Have the children stand back while you do this so they won't breathe in the dust. You'll need enough concrete mix to fill the lid to about 2 inches from the top. Don't worry about being too exact. You can make more, if needed, or use the extra for stepping-stones.
4. Have the children add water a little bit at a time, mixing it in gently with the trowels. Add just enough water to dampen the concrete thoroughly. It should be dry enough that you can form a ball with it.
5. Guide the children in filling the garbage lid mold with the concrete mixture to about 1 inch depth. Place the chicken wire or hardware cloth on the concrete, pressing firmly so it stays in place. Put another inch of concrete on top of the wire. (The wire will add strength to the birdbath.)

6. Set the garbage can upright inside the lid and in the middle of the concrete. Push down hard, so that the concrete starts to come up around the garbage can.
7. Using the hose, fill the garbage can one-quarter full with water. As you fill the garbage can, the weight should push the concrete down even further, making a well in the middle of the birdbath and forming the rim.
8. Fill in any empty areas of the lid with concrete and smooth the edges.
9. Let the children decorate the outside rim of the birdbath with the objects you have selected, pushing them firmly in to the concrete.

10. Remove the garbage can after the concrete has set for about an hour and is able to hold its shape. Let the children decorate the inside of the birdbath.
11. Cover the concrete loosely with plastic wrap so that it will dry slowly. Let the birdbath dry for three days before removing from the mold. Place the finished birdbath in the garden on a tree stump or other pedestal.

### Extensions

Have children clean and fill the birdbath regularly. Encourage them to record observations of birds that visit the birdbath in the form of charts, sketches, photographs, and narratives.

### Safety Considerations

- Be careful not to breathe in the concrete dust.
- Adults and children should wear gloves and dust masks when handling the concrete, as it can be irritating to the skin.
- Children who are still consistently putting sensory materials in their mouths should not participate in this activity.

## A-B-C You in the Garden

*Concepts*

⊛ Garden plants have a variety of names.

⊛ All books have a common format (such as cover, title page, binding)

⊛ Gardens require a variety of tools, materials, and equipment—these all have names.

*Materials*

three-ring binder or fastening brads
26 pieces of paper with one alphabet letter on each page
three-hole-punch
garden magazines or seed catalogs
photographs of plants in your garden
crayons or colored pencils
scissors
glue or tape
camera or extra garden photos
garden alphabet books (see appendix 1)

*Description*

1. Prepare by placing materials on a table. Read a garden-related alphabet book to a group of children before inviting them to make their own garden alphabet book. Explain that this book can be about anything needed to take care of a garden or any plants you have in your current garden.

2. Assist the children in creating a cover for the book and a title page with the title, authors' names, and "publisher" (such as the name of your school or class).

3. Allow each child to choose a letter of the alphabet (such as the first letter of their first name).

4. Encourage the children to think of a plant, garden tool, creature, or activity that they have seen in the garden. For example, they might think of ants for the letter *A*, bulbs for the letter *B*, and coneflower for the letter *C*.

5. Have each child write the word they choose on their letter page. If some children cannot write, write the words for them. You could also show them how to type and print the word at the computer to cut and paste to their page.

6. Allow the children to a cut a picture of the object that their plant- or garden-related word represents from the garden catalogs and magazines. If pictures are not available, the children can draw their own or use an instant or digital camera to take a photo for their page. Double prints of the photos you may have taken for your garden journal also work well for this project.

7. Once each child has drawn or glued his picture, he can either look for another item that begins with that letter or start a new alphabet page.

8. Once the glue has dried and all pages are complete, bind them together in a three-ring binder or fasten them using brass brads. If you do not have a three-hole-punch, magnetic photo albums make nice books and help you avoid the wait for glue to dry.

9. Place the finished book in the reading area and encourage the "authors" to read it to other children, parents, and guests throughout the week.

*Extensions*

With a small group of children, take a set of alphabet cards out to the garden (one letter on each card with a picture to illustrate the letter, such as *A* is for alligator) for an alphabet scavenger hunt. Give each child a card and challenge him to find a plant or garden item that begins with that letter. For example, *D* is for dirt, *S* is for Sprinkler, *Z* is for zinnias. If children want, you can add these discoveries as new pages to the alphabet book.

# 8

# Recipes

We have included some of our favorite recipes below. These include recipes for gardening, such as potting soil and insect sprays, as well as for foods and garden crafts.

## Recipes for the Garden

 *Potting Soil*

You can purchase topsoil from any garden center. Use the kind that comes in a bag if you want to prevent the problem of weed seeds. Another recipe for potting soil, along with more detailed directions, can be found in chapter 6, "Soiled Again."

1 part topsoil
1 part compost
1 part perlite

1. Mix ingredients together in a large tub or sensory table.

2. Moisten thoroughly before planting.

### ✳ *Garlic Bug Spray*

> 5 cloves garlic
> 1 quart water
> cheesecloth

1. Mash garlic cloves and remove skin.

2. Add garlic to water. Let sit overnight.

3. Strain garlic water through cheesecloth. Pour into spray bottle. Use to spray pesky insects.


### ✳ *Soap Bug Spray*

> ½ cup liquid soap
> 1 gallon water

1. Gently mix soap with water, so as not to make too many bubbles.

2. Pour mixture into spray bottles and spray on pests.


### ✳ *Garlic and Soap Bug Spray*

> 1 quart hot water
> 4 cloves garlic
> 2 tablespoons liquid soap
> cheesecloth

1. Crush and peel the garlic.

2. Add the garlic to the hot water. Gently stir in the soap so that it doesn't bubble too much.

3. Let sit overnight.

4. Strain the mixture through the cheesecloth and pour into spray bottles. Spray on bothersome bugs.


### ✳ *Slug Trap*

> 1 tablespoon dry yeast
> ¼ cup sugar
> 3 cups warm water

1. Mix the yeast and sugar in the warm water.

2. Place a shallow can or pan with straight sides in the problem area of the garden. (Tuna cans or old baking pans work well for this. The goal is for the slugs to be able to get in, but not out.)

3. Fill the pan with the yeast mixture. Check the next morning to see if you have caught any slugs.

# Recipes for Eating

## ✿ *Purple Pansy Pumpernickel Sandwiches*

These sandwiches are beautiful and we like to make them for family events. Despite the name, which we love to repeat, we also use other flavors of bread and other colors of pansies when we make them. You can also use nasturtiums.

1 loaf thinly sliced cocktail bread
8 ounces cream cheese spread
fresh pansies, washed and cut directly
 under the flower

For each sandwich, cover one piece of cocktail bread with cream cheese spread. Place a pansy flower on top.

## ✿ *Butter*

When the butter is ready you can clearly differentiate between the butter and the liquid. If the cream is frothy, it is not ready.

1 cup whipping cream (heavy cream)

1. Place cream in a pint jar with a tight-fitting lid. Place the lid on the jar.
2. Shake the jar until the liquid separates from the fat. (This will take some time, so you might want to pass the jar around.)
3. Pour the liquid buttermilk off the butter.

## ✿ *Flower Butter*

Homemade butter or 1 stick (½ cup) store-bought butter
2 tablespoons honey
¼ cup edible flower petals (pansies, nasturtiums, and violets are good choices)

1. Leave butter at room temperature until it is very soft.
2. While the butter softens, prepare the flower petals by washing thoroughly and dry them by placing between paper towels. If the flower petals are very small, use them as they are. If they are from larger flowers, have the children cut them into small pieces with clean scissors.
3. With a wooden spoon, stir the honey into the butter.
4. Gently stir the flower petals into the mixture.

## Cooking with Flowers

Cooking with flowers is fun, especially since so few people know that many flowers are edible. However, with young children, cooking with flowers requires the teacher to be active in educating children about what flowers can and cannot be eaten. Since children cannot be expected to be plant experts, they need to be instructed to only eat flowers when adults say it is safe.

Adults should keep in mind the following guidelines for cooking with flowers:

• Eat only flowers you know are edible.
• Remember that some flowers are poisonous. If you aren't certain about a flower's identity, don't eat it.
• Eat only the petals of flowers. Remove pistils and stamens.
• Eat flowers only if you know they have been grown without the use of pesticides. (For this reason, never eat commercially grown flowers.)

To learn all about cooking with flowers, read *Edible Flowers: From Garden to Palate* (Barash 1995).

## Edible Flowers

Always be sure that flowers are edible before eating or cooking with them. These are just a few flowers that are edible:

pansy
nasturtium
daylily
violet
calendula
chive
mint
rose*
signet marigold
dandelion

*Never eat purchased roses. They almost certainly have been treated with pesticides and fungicides. For this reason, children should not play with petals from florist roses either. If you use roses for cooking projects, be sure that they have not been sprayed.

### ⊛ Herb Butter

Homemade butter or 1 stick (½ cup) store-bought butter
¼ cup fresh herbs, loosely packed (chives, basil, dill, and parsley are good choices)

1. Leave butter at room temperature until it is very soft.

2. Clean and chop the herbs.

3. Using a fork, mix the herbs into the butter. Spread on crackers to serve.

### ⊛ Fried Green Tomatoes

4 medium tomatoes
⅔ cup cornmeal
1 teaspoon salt
½ teaspoon pepper
3 tablespoons oil

1. Use tomatoes that have reached their full size, but have not yet turned red. Slice the tomatoes into pieces about ½-inch thick. Pat the slices dry.

2. Combine the cornmeal, salt, and pepper in a shallow dish, such as a pie plate.

3. Coat the tomatoes thoroughly with the cornmeal mixture.

4. Heat the oil in a skillet until very hot.

5. Fry the tomatoes until brown (about 1½ minutes). Turn. Repeat on other side.

6. Drain on paper towels before eating.

### ⊛ Mini Pizzas

English muffins (one half per pizza)
pizza or spaghetti sauce
vegetables such as tomatoes, onions, and green peppers
mozzarella cheese

1. Preheat oven to 400 degrees F.

2. Prepare vegetables by cleaning and cutting into small pieces.

3. For each pizza, use an English muffin half, cut crosswise. Place 1 tablespoon pizza or spaghetti sauce on the muffin half and spread to the edges.

4. Sprinkle some vegetables on top of the sauce.

5. Sprinkle about 1 tablespoon mozzarella cheese on top of the vegetables.

6. Bake in oven for about ten minutes until the cheese is melted.

## Basil-Tomato Pie

1 9-inch frozen piecrust
1 cup dry beans
2 cups (8 ounces) shredded mozzarella cheese
8 medium tomatoes or 2 cups cherry tomatoes
3 large or 5 small cloves garlic
1 cup fresh basil leaves, loosely packed
½ cup mayonnaise
⅓ cup Parmesan cheese

1. Preheat oven to 450 degrees F.

2. Let piecrust thaw at room temperature about fifteen minutes. Do not prick crust. Place a piece of aluminum foil over crust and fill with dry beans to keep the crust from puffing in the center. Bake for five minutes. Carefully remove beans and foil. (Beans can be saved for other projects.) Return to the oven for another five minutes. When you remove the crust, reduce the oven temperature to 375 degrees F.

3. While still hot, sprinkle ¾ cup of the mozzarella cheese over the crust.

4. Cut tomatoes in wedges and remove core and seeds. Place over cheese in pie crust.

5. Chop basil leaves and garlic until fine. (You can use a food processor or blender for this.) Sprinkle over the tomatoes.

6. Mix mayonnaise with the Parmesan cheese and the remaining 1¼ cup of mozzarella cheese. Spread over the tomatoes and basil.

7. Bake, uncovered for twenty-five minutes or until the cheese is bubbly.


## Basil-Cream Pasta

5 cloves garlic
¼ to ⅓ cup olive oil
2 cups fresh basil leaves, loosely packed
2 cups half-and-half
1 cup fresh grated parmesan cheese
1 pound rotini pasta
salt and pepper to taste

1. Peel the garlic cloves. Put them with 2 tablespoons of the olive oil in the blender. With blender on low speed, alternate adding basil leaves and oil until you have used all the basil and you have a green paste.

2. Mix the basil paste with the half-and-half and the Parmesan cheese in a saucepan. Heat over low heat just until the sauce is hot.

3. Cook the rotini following the package directions.

4. Drain the rotini and mix with the sauce. Add salt and pepper to taste.

### ✸ Salsa

We keep our salsa mild. You can substitute chili peppers for the green bell or banana peppers to liven it up.

2 tablespoons onion, chopped
2 large or 4 small tomatoes
½ green bell pepper or 2 banana peppers, chopped
½ sweet red pepper (optional)
1 tablespoon parsley
1 tablespoon cilantro
1 teaspoon lemon juice

1. Mix all ingredients. Let sit for at least thirty minutes to allow flavors to blend.

2. Serve with tortilla chips.

### ✸ Coleslaw

1 medium head of cabbage
2 carrots
1 cup coleslaw dressing
1 teaspoon celery seed

1. Clean and grate the cabbage and carrots. Place in a large bowl.

2. Mix the cabbage and carrots with the coleslaw dressing and celery seed. Stir well to coat the cabbage and carrots thoroughly.

### ✸ Marigold Cheesecake

3 8-ounce packages cream cheese, softened
1¼ cup sugar
3 tablespoons flour
2 teaspoons grated lemon peel
3 tablespoons chopped marigold petals
1 tablespoon chopped mint or lemon balm leaves
¼ teaspoon vanilla
6 eggs
2 tablespoons heavy cream

1. Preheat oven to 425 degrees F.

2. In a large bowl, beat the cream cheese with a wooden spoon.

3. Blend in the sugar, flour, lemon peel, marigold petals, mint or lemon balm, and vanilla.

4. Add the eggs, one at a time, beating thoroughly after each egg.

5. Stir in the cream.

6. Pour into a greased 9-inch springform pan. Place pan on a baking sheet and place in oven. Bake for fifteen minutes at 425 degrees F. Reduce oven temperature to 250 degrees F and continue to bake for another hour until golden brown.

7. Remove from oven and cool for one hour before removing sides of pan. Garnish with marigold blossoms and lemon zest or mint to serve.

## *Herb Tea*

fresh herbs, such as mint, lemon balm, or chamomile
water

1. Pick and wash the herb leaves. Measure out ½ cup of leaves, loosely packed. Place in a 1-quart pitcher.

2. Add two cups boiling water to the herb leaves. Let sit for five minutes.

3. Add ice and cold water to fill the pitcher. Strain to serve.


## *Chive Potato Pancakes*

½ cup sour cream
2 tablespoons plus ½ cup fresh chives, chopped
1 tablespoons Dijon-style prepared mustard
6 medium-size potatoes, peeled
¼ cup flour
½ teaspoon baking powder
½ teaspoon salt
¼ teaspoon black pepper
¼ cup vegetable oil, for frying

1. To make sauce, in a small bowl, combine the sour cream and the mustard with 2 tablespoons of the chives. Cover and refrigerate until ready to serve.

2. Grate the potatoes, using a hand grater or a food processor. Discard any liquid that gathers.

3. In a large bowl, combine the potatoes with the flour, baking powder, salt, pepper, and ½ cup chives. Stir until well blended.

4. Pour oil into skillet. When oil is hot, drop the batter into it, using about ¼ cup of the mixture for each pancake. Flatten slightly and cook until golden brown on bottom (about five minutes). Turn and cook until the underside is brown. Drain well.

5. Serve with sour cream sauce.


## *Sun Tea*

2 large tea bags
½ cup herbs, such as mints, lemon balm, lemon verbena, or chamomile
water

1. Wrap the herbs in a square of muslin and tie with a string. Place the tea bags and the packet of herbs in a 1-gallon clear jar.

2. Fill the jar with water.

3. Place the jar in the sun and let it sit for four to six hours until the tea has brewed.

# Recipes for Fun

✳ *Herb Bath Sachets*

Fresh or dried herbs
6-inch square of muslin
string

1. Place the herbs in the center of the muslin.

2. Gather the cloth around the herbs. Tie with the string.

3. Add to bath water for a pleasant scent.

## Herbs for Sachets and Potpourri

basil
chamomile
scented geranium
English lavender
lemon balm
lemon verbena
mints
rosemary
lemon thyme
peppermint
pineapple sage
spearmint
sweet woodruff

✳ *Sachets*

dried herb leaves and flowers
dried lemon or orange peel
small bowl
6-inch square muslin and string or two 4-inch squares of fabric, needle, and thread
glue
small dried flowers
ribbon pieces

1. Mix the herb leaves, flowers, and dried citrus peel.

2. For non-sewers, use the large piece of muslin. Place about 2 tablespoons of the herb mixture in the middle of the square of muslin. Gather the fabric around the herbs and tie with the string. If your children can sew, have them use the smaller 4-inch pieces of fabric. Place the fabric pieces back to back and sew around three sides. Fill with herb mixture before sewing the fourth side.

3. Glue small dried flowers and ribbon to the outside of the sachet for decoration.

# Appendix 1

## Children's Books about Gardens and Garden Creatures

### Fiction

Barner, Bob. *Bugs! Bugs! Bugs!* New York: Scholastic, 1999.

Bunting, Eve. *Sunflower House*. New York: Harcourt, Brace, 1996.

Bunting, Eve, and Kathryn Hewitt. *Flower Garden*. New York: Scholastic, 1994.

Cole, Henry. *Jack's Garden*. New York: Greenwillow Books, 1995.

Cole, Joanna, and Bruce Degen. *The Magic School Bus Gets Ants in Its Pants: A Book About Ants*. New York: Scholastic, 1996.

Ehlert, Lois. *Planting a Rainbow*. New York: Scholastic, 1988.

Facklam, Margery, and Sylvia Long. *Bugs for Lunch*. New York: Scholastic, 1999.

Finch, Mary, and Elisabeth Bell. *The Little Red Hen and the Ear of Wheat*. Brooklyn: Barefoot Books, Inc, 1999.

Guest, C. Z., and Loretta Krupinski. *Tiny Green Thumbs*. New York: Scholastic, 2000.

Heiligman, Deborah, and Bari Weissman. *From Caterpillar to Butterfly*. New York: Scholastic, 1998.

Kraus, Ruth. *The Carrot Seed*. New York: Harper Collins Publishers, 1973.

Lin, Grace. *The Ugly Vegetables*. Watertown, Mass.: Charlesbridge Publishing, 1999.

Mallett, David, and Ora Eitan. *Inch by Inch: The Garden Song*. New York: Harper Collins Publishers, 1995.

Mazzola Jr., Frank. *Counting Is for the Birds*. New York: Scholastic, 1997.

McDonald, Margaret Read, and Pat Cummings. *Pickin' Peas*. New York: Harper Collins Publishers, 1998.

Oram, Hiawyn, and Susan Varley. *Princess Chamomile's Garden*. New York: Dutton Children's Books, 2000.

Pinczes, Elinor J. *One Hundred Hungry Ants*. New York: Houghton Mifflin, 1993.

Rockwell, Anne. *Bumblebee, Bumblebee, Do You Know Me? A Garden Guessing Game*. New York: Scholastic, 1999.

Rockwell, Anne, and Megan Halsey. *One Bean*. New York: Scholastic, 1998.

Rylant, Cynthia, and Mary Szilagyi. *This Year's Garden*. New York: Aladdin Paperbacks, 1984.

Stewart, Sarah, and David Small. *The Gardener*. New York: Farrar, Straus and Giroux, 1997.

Van Allsburg, Chris. *Two Bad Ants*. New York: Houghton Mifflin, 1998.

## Nonfiction

Brennan, Patricia. *Those Amazing Ants*. New York: Simon and Schuster, 1994.

Burne, David. *Eyewitness Books: Bird*. New York: Dorling Kindersley, 2000.

———. *Eyewitness Books: Plant*. New York: Dorling Kindersley, 2000.

Canizares, Susan, and Daniel Moreton. *Who Lives in a Tree?* New York: Scholastic, 1998. *

Canizares, Susan, and Mary Reid. *Where Do Insects Live?* New York: Scholastic, 1998. *

Canizares, Susan, and Pamela Chanko. *What Do Insects Do?* New York: Scholastic, 1998.*

Coughlan, Cheryl. *Ants*. Mankato, Minn.: Capstone Press, 1999. *

———. *Bumble Bees*. Mankato, Minn.: Capstone Press, 1999. *

———. *Ladybugs*. Mankato, Minn.: Capstone Press, 1999. *

Dorros, Arthur. *Ant Cities*. New York: Scholastic, 1987.

Gibbons, Gail. *Spiders*. New York: Scholastic, 1993.

Gjersvik, Marianne Haug. *Green Fun: Plants as Play*. Ontario, Canada: Firefly Books, 1997.

Glaser, Linda, and Anca Hariton. *Compost! Growing Gardens from Your Garbage*. Brookfield, Conn.: The Millbrook Press, 1996.

Greenaway, Theresa, and Chris Fairclough. *Beetles*. Austin, Tex.: Raintree Steck-Vaughn, 1999.

———. *Slugs and Snails*. Austin, Tex.: Raintree Steck-Vaughn, 1999.

———. *Worms*. Austin, Tex.: Raintree Steck-Vaughn, 1999.

Grossman, Patricia. *Very First Things to Know About Ants*. New York: Workman Publishing, 1997.

Hickman, Pamela, and Heather Collins. *A Seed Grows: My First Look at a Plant's Life Cycle*. Ontario, Canada: Kids Can Press, 1997.

Holmes, Kevin J. *Bees*. Mankato, Minn.: Capstone Press, 1998. *

———. *Butterflies*. Mankato, Minn.: Capstone Press, 1998. *

———. *Earthworms*. Mankato, Minn.: Capstone Press, 1998. *

Krementz, Jill. *A Very Young Gardener*. New York: Dial Books for Young Readers, 1991.

Lavies, Biana. *Compost Critters*. New York: Children's Books, 1993.

Martin, Alexander C. *Weeds*. New York: Golden Books, 1987.

Mauno, Laurence. *Eyewitness Books: Insect*. New York: Dorling Kindersley, 2000.

McLaughlin, Molly. *Earthworms, Dirt, and Rotten Leaves*. New York: Atheneum, 1986.

Mitchell, Robert T., and Herbert S. Zim. *Butterflies and Moths: A Guide to the More Common American Species*. New York: Golden Books, 1987.

Mound, Laurence. *Insect*. New York: Alfred A. Knopf, 1990.

Nicholas, Christopher, and Nike Maydak. *Bugs! (Know-It-Alls)*. New York: McClanahan Books, 1998.

Parker, Nancy Winslow, and Joan Richards Wright. *Bugs*. New York: Scholastic, 1987.

Reid, Mary, and Betsey Chessen. *Bugs, Bugs, Bugs!* New York: Scholastic, 1998.*

Rosen, Michael J. *Down to Earth*. New York: Harcourt, Brace, 1998.

Saunders-Smith, Gail. *Flowers*. Mankato, Minn.: Capstone Press, 1998. *

————. *Sunflowers*. Mankato, Minn.: Capstone Press, 1998. *

Schaufer, Lola M. *Honey Bees and Flowers*. Mankato, Minn.: Capstone Press, 1999. *

Whalley, Paul. *Eyewitness Books: Butterfly and Moth*. New York: Dorling Kindersley, 2000.

Wilsdon, Christina. *National Audubon Society First Field Guide: Insects*. New York: Scholastic, 1998.

Wolff, Ferida, and Janet Pedersen. *A Weed Is a Seed*. New York: Houghton Mifflin, 1996.

Zim, Herbert S., and Ira N. Gabrielson. *Birds: A Guide to Familiar Birds of North America*. New York: Golden Books, 1987.

Zim, Herbert S., and Alexander C. Martin. *Flowers: A Guide to Familiar American Wildflowers*. New York: Golden Books, 1987.

Zim, Herbert S., and Clarence Cottam. *Insects: A Guide to Familiar American Insects*. New York: Golden Books, 1987.

## Alphabet Books

Christenson, Bonnie. *An Edible Alphabet*. New York: Dial Books for Young Readers, 1994.

Ehlert, Lois. *Eating the Alphabet: Fruits and Vegetables from A to Z*. New York: Harcourt, 1993.

Pallotta, Jerry. *The Flower Alphabet Book*. Watertown, Mass.: Charlesbridge Publishing, 1988.

Sandved, Kjell B. *The Butterfly Alphabet*. New York: Scholastic, 1996.

Tillett, Leslie. *Plant and Animal Alphabet Coloring Book*. Mineola, N.Y.: Dover Publications, 1980.

Wilner, Isabel. *A Garden Alphabet*. New York: Dutton Children's Books, 1991.

*An asterisk denotes a book with very simple text. These would be appropriate for infants and toddlers, but also have excellent photographs that make them useful with older children.

# Appendix 2

## Reference Books about Garden Creatures

Appelhof, Mary. *Worms Eat My Garbage*. Kalamazoo, Mich.: Flower Press, 1982.

Cohen, Richard, and Betty Phillips Tunick. *Snail Trails and Tadpole Tales*. St. Paul: Redleaf Press, 1993.

Durrell, Gerald. *A Practical Guide for the Amateur Naturalist*. New York: Alfred A. Knopf, 1982.

Kramer, David C. *Animals in the Classroom*. Reading, Mass.: Addison-Wesley, 1989.

Lavies, Bianca. *Compost Critters*. New York: Dutton Children's Books, 1993.

Lowenstein, Frank, and Sheryl Lechner. *Bugs: Insects, Spiders, Centipedes, Millipedes, and Other Closely Related Arthropods*. New York: Black Dog and Leventhal Publishers, 1999.

Mitchell, Robert T., and Herbert S. Zim. *Butterflies and Moths*. New York: Golden Press, 1987.

Ross, Michael Elsohn. *Snailology*. Minneapolis: Carolrhoda Books, Inc., 1996.

———. *Wormology*. Minneapolis: Carolrhoda Books, Inc., 1996.

———. *Caterpillarology*. Minneapolis: Carolrhoda Books, Inc., 1997.

Starcher, Allison Mia. *Good Bugs for Your Garden*. Chapel Hill, N.C.: Algonquin Books of Chapel Hill, 1998.

# Appendix 3

## Garden and Environmental Educational Books and Supplies

*Including Sources for Insects, Worms, and Other Beneficial Creatures*

Acorn Naturalists
17821 East 17th Street, Suite 103
Tustin, CA 92780
800-422-8886
www.acornnaturalists.com

The Bug Store
113 West Argonne
St. Louis, MO 63122-1104
800-455-2847
www.bugstore.com

Gardening With Kids
National Gardening Association
180 Flynn Ave.
Burlington, VT 05401
800-538-7476
www.kidsgardening.com

Gardens Alive
5100 Schenley Place
Lawrenceburg, IN 47025
812-537-8650
www.gardens-alive.com

Insect Lore
P.O. Box 1535
Shafter, CA 93263
800-LIVE-BUG

Kids in Bloom
P.O. Box 344
Zionsville, IN 46077
317-290-6996

Lakeshore Learning Materials
2695 East Dominguez Street
Carson, CA. 90749
800-421-5354
www.lakeshorelearning.com

Let's Get Growing
1900 Commercial Way
Santa Cruz, CA 95065
800-408-1868
www.letsgetgrowing.com

NASCO
901 Janesville Avenue
P.O. Box 901
Fort Atkinson, WI 53538-1901
800-558-9595
www.enasco.com

Resources for Garden-based Education
Gardens for Growing People
P.O. Box 630
Point Reyes Station, CA 94956
415-663-9433
www.svn.net/growpepl

# Appendix 4

## Seeds and Garden Supplies

Burpee
W. Atlee Burpee & Co.
Warminster, PA 18974
800-888-1447
www.burpee.com

The Cook's Garden
P.O. Box 535
Londonderry, VT 05148
www.cooksgarden.com

The Gardener's Supply Company
128 Intervale Road
Burlington, VT 05401
800-863-1700
www.gardeners.com

Johnny's Selected Seeds
Foss Hill Road
RR 1, Box 2580
Albion, ME 04910-9731
www.johnnyseeds.com

Park Seed
George W. Park Seed Co., Inc.
1 Parkton Avenue
Greenwood, SC 29647-0001
800-845-3369
www.parkseed.com

Peaceful Valley Farm Supply
P.O. Box 2209
Grass Valley, CA 95945
888-784-1722
www.groworganic.com

Select Seeds: Antique Flowers
180 Stickney Hill Road
Union, CT 06076-4617
860-684-9310
www.selectseeds.com

Seeds of Change
P.O. Box 15700
Santa Fe, NM 87506-5700
www.seedsofchange.com

Shepherd's Garden Seeds
30 Irene Street
Torrington, CT 06790-6658
860-482-3638
www.shepherdseeds.com

Territorial Seed Company
P.O. Box 158
Cottage Grove, OR 97424-0061
541-942-9547
www.territorial-seed.com

Thompson and Morgan
P.O. Box 1308
Jackson, NJ 08527-0308
www.thompson-morgan.com

Totally Tomatoes
P.O. Box 1626
Augusta, GA 30903-1626
803-663-0016
www.totallytomato.com

Wildseed Farms
425 Wildflower Hills
P.O. Box 3000
Fredericksburg, TX 48624-3000
www.wildseedfarms.com

# Appendix 5

## Common and Botanical Names of Plants Mentioned

| Common Name | Botanical Name |
| --- | --- |
| Amaryllis | *Hippeastrum* hybrids |
| Angel's trumpet | *Brugmansia arborea* |
| Astilbe | *Astilbe arendsii* |
| Azalea | *Rhododendron* species |
| Banana pepper | *Capsicum* Anaheim 'banana' |
| Barberry | *Berberis* |
| Basil | *Ocimum basilicum* |
| Bean | *Phaseolus vulgaris* |
| Bee balm | *Monarda didyma* |
| Belladonna | *Atropa belladonna* |
| Bermuda grass | *Cynodon dactylon* |
| Blackberry | *Rubus* species |
| Blanketflower | *Gaillardia x grandiflora* |
| Bleeding heart | *Dicentra spectablis* |
| Blueberry | *Vaccinium* species |
| Blue salvia | *Salvia farinacea* |
| Broccoli | *Brassica oleracea* (Italica group) |
| Buttercup | *Primula floribunda* |

| | |
|---|---|
| Butterfly bush | *Buddleia davidii* |
| Cabbage | *Brassica oleracea* (capitata group) |
| Cauliflower | *Brassica oleracea* (botrytis group) |
| Canna | *Canna-hybrida* |
| Carrot | *Daucus carota* |
| Castor bean | *Ricinus communis* |
| Chamomile | *Chamaemelum nobilis* |
| Chinese lantern | *Physalis alkengii* |
| Chocolate mint | *Mentha* species |
| Cockscomb | *Celosia argentea* |
| Columbine | *Aquilegia* hybrid |
| Coreopsis | *Coreopsis tinctoria* |
| Corn | *Zea mays* |
| Cosmos | *Cosmos bipinnatus* |
| Crocus | *Crocus sativus* |
| Cucumber | *Cucumis sativus* |
| Daffodil | *Narcissus* species |
| Dahlia | *Dahlia* species |
| Dusty miller | *Senecio cineraria* |
| Eggplant | *Solanum* 'Dusky' |
| English Ivy | *Hedera helix* |
| Ferns | *Matteuccia* variety |
| Foxglove | *Digitalis* |
| Garlic | *Allium sativum* |
| Geranium | *Pelargonium* species |
| Ginkgo | *Ginkgo biloba* |
| Gourd | *Cucurbita pepo* |
| Gourd, birdhouse | *Lagenaria* species |
| Grasses that rustle | *Chasmanthium latifolum* |
| Green beans | *Phaseolus vulgaris* |
| Green pepper | *Capsicum annuum* |
| Hollyhock | *Alcea rosea* |
| Hosta | *Hosta* species |
| Hyacinth | *Hyacinthus* species |
| Impatiens | *Impatiens* species |
| Indigo | *Indigofera* species |
| Iris | *Iris* species |
| Jonquil | *Narcissus* species |
| Lamb's ear | *Stachys byzantina* |
| Lemon mint | *Mentha citrata* |
| Lettuce | *Lactuca sativa* |
| Lilac | *Syringa patula* |
| Lime mint | *Mentha citrata* |
| Marigold | *Tagetes* |
| Melon | *Cucumis melo* |
| Money plant | *Lunaria annua* |
| Mum | *Chrysanthemum* species |

| | |
|---|---|
| Nasturtiums | *Tropaeolum majus* |
| Nutsedge | *Cyperus esculentus* |
| Onion | *Allium* species |
| Oregano | *Origanum dictamnus* |
| Pansy | *Viola* species |
| Paperwhite narcissus | *Narcissus* |
| Parsley | *Petroselinum crispum* |
| Pinks | *Dianthus* species |
| Popcorn | *Zea mays* V. *everta* |
| Potato | *Solanum tuberosum* |
| Pumpkin | *Cucurbita pepo* |
| Radish | *Raphanus sativus* |
| Red salvia | *Salvia* species |
| Sage | *Salvia officinalis* |
| Sedum | *Sedum* species |
| Shrub rose | *Rosa gallica* |
| Snapdragon | *Antirrhinum majus* |
| Spinach | *Spinacia oleracea* |
| Squash | *Cucurbita pepo* |
| Statice | *Limonium sinuatum* |
| Strawberry | *Fragaria* species |
| Strawflower | *Helichrysum bracteatum* |
| Sweet alyssum | *Lobularia maritime* |
| Tansy | *Tanacetum vulgare* |
| Thyme | *Thymus vulgaris* |
| Tomato | *Lycopersicon* |
| Tulip | *Tulipa* species |
| Zinnia | *Zinnia* species |

# Appendix 6

## Poisonous Plants

| Common Name | Botanical Name | Toxic Parts | Symptoms |
|---|---|---|---|
| Autumn crocus | *Colchicum autumnale* | All parts, particularly the bulb | Burning sensation in the mouth, vomiting, nausea, and severe diarrhea. |
| Azaleas | *Rhododendron* species | All parts, particularly leaves and flowers | Nausea, vomiting, depression, difficulty breathing, low blood pressure, and convulsions; can be fatal. |
| Bittersweet | *Solanum dulcamara* | Leaves, roots, and berries | Vomiting, nausea, abdominal pain, diarrhea, drowsiness, tremors, and weakness. May cause difficulty in breathing. |
| Black locust | *Robinia pseudoacacia* | Bark, leaves, and seeds | Burning pain in the mouth, abdominal pain, nausea, vomiting, severe diarrhea. |
| Bleeding heart | *Dicentra spectabilis* | Foliage and roots | May be poisonous in large amounts. |
| Caladium | *Caladium* species | All parts | Intense burning and irritation of the mouth, tongue, throat, and lips. Swollen lips and tongue; can cause suffocation. |

| Common Name | Botanical Name | Toxic Parts | Symptoms |
|---|---|---|---|
| Calla lily | Zantedeschia i | All parts, especially the leaves and root | Intense burning of the lips and mouth. |
| Castor bean | Ricinus communis | Seed, if chewed (toxic substance: ricin) | Burning sensation in the mouth, abdominal pain, nausea, vomiting, severe diarrhea, and kidney failure. Can be fatal. |
| Christmas rose | Helleborus niger | All parts | Stomach, intestinal, and skin irritation. |
| Crown-of-thorns | Euphorbia milii | All parts | Intense burning and irritation of the mouth, tongue, throat, and lips; swollen lips and tongue; skin and eye irritation. |
| Daffodil | Narcissus | Bulbs | Stomach pain, vomiting, abdominal pain, and diarrhea. |
| Daphne | Daphne | All parts, especially berries, bark, and leaves (toxic substance: daphnin) | Burning of the mouth and throat, abdominal pain, vomiting, diarrhea, and kidney damage. Can be fatal. |
| Dieffenbachia, Dumbcane | Dieffenbachia species | All parts | Intense burning and irritation of the mouth, tongue, throat, and lips; swollen lips and tongue. Can cause suffocation. |
| Elderberry | Sambucus | Stems, roots, and unripe or raw berries (ripe berries are edible) | Nausea, vomiting, and diarrhea. |
| Elephant ears | Colocasia species | Leaves | Intense burning and irritation of the mouth, tongue, throat, and lips; swollen lips and tongue. Can cause suffocation. |
| English ivy | Hedera helix | All parts, especially berries and leaves | Excess salivation, nausea, vomiting, thirst, severe diarrhea, and abdominal pain. May cause difficulty in breathing. |
| Foxglove | Digitalis | All parts, especially leaves, seeds, and flowers | Stomach pain, nausea, vomiting, abdominal pain, diarrhea, and irritation of mouth. May produce an irregular heart beat. May be fatal. |
| Golden chain | Laburnum | All parts, especially bark, leaves, and seeds | Abdominal pains, nausea, vomiting, headache, dizziness, skin and mouth irritation, and convulsions. May be fatal. |
| Hyacinth | Hyacinthus species | All parts, especially bulbs | Vomiting, abdominal pain, and diarrhea. Can be fatal. |

| Common Name | Botanical Name | Toxic Parts | Symptoms |
|---|---|---|---|
| Holly | *Ilex aquifolium* | Berries | Nausea, vomiting, abdominal pain, and diarrhea. |
| Iris | *Iris* | Leaves and roots | Stomach pain, nausea, vomiting, abdominal pain, diarrhea, and burning of the mouth. |
| Jack-in-the-pulpit | *Arisaema triphyllum* | All parts, especially leaves | Intense burning of the mouth, tongue, throat, and lips; swollen lips and tongue. May interfere with speaking, swallowing. or breathing. |
| Japanese yew | *Taxus cuspidata* | Leaves and seeds | Abdominal pain, vomiting. In severe cases, muscular weakness, and cardiac and respiratory disturbances. |
| Jasmine | *Jasminum officinale* | Berries | Digestive and nervous symptoms. Can be fatal. |
| Jerusalem cherry | *Solanum pseudocapsicum* | All parts, especially leaves and fruit (unripe fruit) | Nausea, vomiting, abdominal pain, diarrhea, dilation of pupils, and drowsiness. |
| Lantana | *Lantana* | All parts, especially the green berries | Stomach upset, vomiting, diarrhea, weakness, visual disturbances. |
| Larkspur | *Delphinium* | Plant seeds | Stomach upset, nervousness, irritability, depression. |
| Lily of the valley | *Convallaria majalis* | All parts, especially roots, leaves, flowers, and fruit | Stomach pain, nausea, vomiting, abdominal pain, and diarrhea; may produce an irregular heart beat. |
| May apple | *Podophyllum peltatum* | Rootstalk, leaves, stems, and green fruit | Abdominal pain, vomiting, diarrhea, and pulse irregularities. |
| Mistletoe | *Phoradendron serotinum* | Leaves, stems, and berries | Vomiting, diarrhea, dilated pupils, confusion; respiratory distress. |
| Monk's hood | *Aconitum napellus* | All parts, especially the root and leaves | Throat congestion, increased salivation, weakness, nausea, vomiting, tingling sensation, skin is cold and moist; poisoning of the system. |
| Moonseed | *Menispermum canadense* | Mature fruit | Convulsions, poisoning of the system. Can be fatal. |
| Morning glory | *Ipomoea purpurea* | All parts, especially seeds | Hallucinations; poisoning of the system. |

| Common Name | Botanical Name | Toxic Parts | Symptoms |
|---|---|---|---|
| Mountain laurel | *Kalmia latifolia* | Leaves, twigs, and flowers | Stomach and intestinal irritation, paralysis, convulsions. |
| Mushroom | Various *Amanita* species | All parts | Edible mushrooms are difficult to distinguish. Poisonous mushroom ingestion symptoms include abdominal pain, vomiting, diarrhea, headaches, difficulty breathing, sweating, lower blood pressure, hallucinations, distorted vision, loss of coordination. |
| Narcissus | *Narcissus poeticus* | Bulbs | Stomach pain, vomiting, abdominal pain, and diarrhea. |
| Nutmeg | *Myristica fragrans* | Seeds | Hallucinations and drowsiness, stomach pain, rapid heart rate, and liver damage. |
| Oak | *Quercus* | Large amounts of raw acorns | Abdominal pain, vomiting, and diarrhea. |
| Oleander | *Nerium oleander* | Leaves, stems, bark, and branches | Stomach pain, vomiting, abdominal pain, diarrhea, and irregularities in the heartbeat. |
| Philodendron | *Philodendron* species | All parts | Intense burning and irritation of the mouth, tongue, throat, and lips; swollen lips and tongue. Can cause suffocation. |
| Poison ivy, Poison oak | *Rhus radicans, Rhus diversilobum* | Sap or oil, found in all parts of the plant (contains urushiols) | Skin irritation, rash, and itchy blisters. |
| Potato | *Solanum tuberosum* | Green tuber, vines, leaves, new sprouts, spoiled parts, new shoots | Ingestion may cause severe vomiting and diarrhea. Do not eat green or spoiled potatoes. |
| Privet, common privet | *Ligustrum vulgare* | Leaves and berries | Nausea, vomiting, abdominal pain, and severe diarrhea. May cause kidney damage. |
| Rhubarb | *Rheum rhaponticum* or *Rheum rhabarbarum* | Berries and leaves (toxic substance: oxalic acid) | Stomach pain, vomiting, abdominal pain, and diarrhea. May cause internal bleeding and convulsions. Can be fatal. |
| Rosary pea | *Abrus precatorius* | Seed, if chewed | Burning in the mouth, abdominal pain, nausea, vomiting, severe diarrhea, and kidney failure. Can be fatal. |

| Common Name | Botanical Name | Toxic Parts | Symptoms |
|---|---|---|---|
| Star of Bethlehem | *Ornithogalum* | Flowers and bulbs | Stomach pain, vomiting, abdominal pain, and diarrhea. |
| Sweet pea | *Lathyrus odoratus* | Seeds | Poisoning of the system, if ingested in large amounts. |
| Tomato | *Lycopersicon, Lycopersicum* | Leaves, vines, and sprouts | Headache, abdominal pain, vomiting, and diarrhea. Can cause circulatory and respiratory depression. |
| Virginia creeper, American ivy | *Parthenocissus gelsemium* | Berries and leaves (toxic substance: oxalic acid) | Nausea, vomiting, abdominal pain, diarrhea, and headache. |
| Wisteria | *Wisterias* | Pods and seeds | Abdominal pain, nausea, vomiting, and diarrhea. |
| Yellow jessamine, Carolina jessamine | *Gelsemium sempervirens* | All parts | Heart arrest, visual disturbances, dizziness, headache, dryness of mouth. Can be fatal. |
| Yellow sage, red sage | *Lantana camara* | Leaves and immature fruit (green berries) | Stomach pain, vomiting, abdominal pain, diarrhea, lethargy, pupil dilation, unconsciousness, difficulty in breathing, weakness. Can be fatal. |

# Index

make-believe. *See* dramatic play
Making the Most of Compost, 123
Mallett, David, 100
mammals, 79–80, 88
manure, 78, 124
Marigold Cheesecake, 154
marigolds
  drying, 117
  in dye gardens, 47
  eating, 46, 152, 154
  and infants/toddlers, 102
  saving seeds, 91
  in sensory gardens, 43
markers, 79
math skills, 4, 98
  graphing, 33–34, 49
  and harvesting, 89
May apple (toxic), 179
McLaughlin, Molly, 136
measuring, 89, 98, 128, 142–143
Measuring Up, 128
melons, 41
memory games, 114, 118
Mexican sage, 46
Mexican tea, 46
Mini Pizzas, 152
mints, 42, 102, 152, 156
misinformation, 24
mistakes, 75
mistletoe (toxic), 179
money plant, 43, 115
monk's hood (toxic), 179
moonseed (toxic), 179
Moore, Robin C., 65–66
morning glory (toxic), 179
motivation. *See* engaging
    children; interest levels
motor skills, 2, 98
mounded-bed gardens
      (berms), 54
  construction, 60–61
Mound, Laurence, 136
mountain laurel (toxic), 180
movement, 2
mulching, 76–77, 126–127
  kitchen gardens, 41
  and motor skills, 2
  and mounded-bed
      gardens, 54, 61
  and planting, 74
Mulch Madness, 126–127
mums, 43
murals, 94
mushrooms, 180
music, 22, 94, 100, 131

N
narcissus (toxic), 180
narrated slide shows, 32
nasturtiums
  eating, 43, 115, 151, 152
  saving seeds, 91
National Gardening Association, 63, 91, 92
Native peoples, 40
nature walks, 22
  rain, 128
  and sensory awareness, 115
  texture, 112
New Guinea impatiens, 45
Nimmo, John, 24
nine-month calendars, 55, 62, 104–105
North American gardens, 40
northern sea oats, 115
nutmeg (toxic seeds), 180

O
observing of children, 7, 13
Ogle, Donna, 22
okra, 46
oleander (toxic), 180
One Step at a Time, 141
onions, 41, 46, 152, 154
open houses, 93
Oram, Hiawyn, 49
oregano, 46

P
pac choi, 46
pansies
  eating, 43, 115, 151, 152
  saving seeds, 91
parent volunteers, 8, 30, 74. *See
    also* adult participation
parsley, 46, 115, 154
parties, 93–94
partners, 75, 103
pasta, 153
paths, 45, 53
patience, 3
peanuts, 46
peas, 91, 104
peat pots, 73
peonies, 117
peppermint, 156
peppers
  in kitchen gardens, 41
  in pizza gardens, 46
  recipes, 152, 154
  saving seeds, 91
perennials vs. annuals, 47, 63–64

pesticides, 80, 81, 150
pests, 80–81, 86–87
*Peter, Paul, and Mommy Too*, 100
Peter Rabbit gardens, 46
philodendron (toxic), 180
photographs
  and building the garden, 58
  and culminating events, 94
  and fieldwork, 30, 31, 32
  and primary-age children, 103
  and seed investigations, 111
  and storyboards, 27
physical development, 2
picking flowers, 2, 44, 78–79, 102
pill bugs, 136–137
pineapple sage, 156
pinks, 39
pizza
  recipe, 152
  and theme gardens, 46, 47
planning, 37–55
  approaches, 48
  bird and butterfly gardens, 37, 39
  and concept webs, 12–14
  dinosaur gardens, 44–45
  garden types, 52–55
  kitchen gardens, 41
  and K-W-L process, 24–25
  layout maps, 38, 39, 40, 41, 42, 45, 47
  North American gardens, 40
  sensory gardens, 42–44
  site selection, 49–52
  subsequent years, 105–106
plant diseases, 81
planting, 2, 71–74
planting depth, 73
plant selection, 63–68
  annuals vs. perennials, 63–64
  and bee allergies, 83
  and climate, 64
  cool weather crops, 104
  and infants/toddlers, 102
  planting seeds, 67–68
  and temperature, 64, 65
  toxic plants, 65–66, 102, 110
  transplants, 66, 68
  *See also* theme gardens
plants, names of, 173–175
*Plants for Play* (Moore), 65–66
plastic pots, 61
poems, 22
poison ivy/oak (toxic), 180
poisonous plants. *See* toxic plants
popcorn, 40

# Other Resources from Redleaf Press

**More Than . . . Series**
*by Sally Moomaw and Brenda Hieronymus*
Six books that make up a child-centered integrated curriculum for five important areas of early learning: math, art, music, science, and literacy. Guaranteed to encourage children to explore, investigate, and discover the wonders of their world!

**Transition Magician: Strategies for Guiding Young Children in Early Childhood Programs**
*by Nola Larson, Mary Henthorne, and Barbara Plum*
Offers over 200 original learning activities that will help teachers smoothly weave everyday activities together.

**Transition Magician 2: More Strategies for Guiding Young Children in Early Childhood Programs**
*by Mary Henthorne, Nola Larson, and Ruth Chvojicek*
More than 200 original learning activities, more than 50 props and games, and adaptations for toddlers and for children with special needs.

**Transition Magician for Families: Helping Parents and Children with Everyday Routines**
*by Ruth Chvojicek, Mary Henthorne, and Nola Larson*
Dozens of activity ideas for caregivers to share with families to simplify the everyday transitions outside of child care.

**Big as Life: The Everyday Inclusive Curriculum, Volumes 1 & 2**
*by Stacey York*
From the author of *Roots and Wings*, these two theme-based curriculum books offer sixteen information-packed units on favorite topics such as *Family, Feelings,* and *Animals.* Each has suggested materials, learning area set-ups, book lists, and loads of activities in all developmental areas. Also includes ideas for field trips, classroom visitors, and activities to counter bias. An essential resource!

**That's Not Fair! A Teacher's Guide to Activism with Young Children**
*by Ann Pelo and Fran Davidson*
Real-life stories of activist children, combined with teachers' experiences and reflections, create a complete guide to children changing their world.

**Focused Portfolios: A Complete Assessment for the Young Child**
*by Gaye Gronlund and Bev Engel*
Offers an innovative way to accurately document children's growth and development by observing them in the midst of their everyday activities. Especially designed for inclusive classrooms.

**Help Yourself! Activities to Promote Safety and Self-Esteem**
by Kate Ross
Contains fun and creative ways to use the songs from the CD *Help Yourself* as a springboard into a curriculum for promoting self-esteem and safety skills among young children.

800-423-8309
www.redleafpress.org